Routledge Revivals

The Psychology of Golf

First published in 1922, *The Psychology of Golf* examines the mental side of golf from the point of view of the player, and the author's whole aim is to assist and interest both the expert and the novice. The game of golf is nine-tenths mental and this book attempts to develop those mental skills in a golf player.

The Psychology of Golf

Leslie Schon

First published in 1922
By Methuen & Co.

This edition first published in 2024 by Routledge
4 Park Square, Milton Park, Abingdon, Oxon, OX14 4RN
and by Routledge
605 Third Avenue, New York, NY 10017

Routledge is an imprint of the Taylor & Francis Group, an informa business

© Methuen & Co., 1922

All rights reserved. No part of this book may be reprinted or reproduced or utilised in any form or by any electronic, mechanical, or other means, now known or hereafter invented, including photocopying and recording, or in any information storage or retrieval system, without permission in writing from the publishers.

Publisher's Note
The publisher has gone to great lengths to ensure the quality of this reprint but points out that some imperfections in the original copies may be apparent.

Disclaimer
The publisher has made every effort to trace copyright holders and welcomes correspondence from those they have been unable to contact.

ISBN: 978-1-032-77090-1 (hbk)
ISBN: 978-1-003-48123-2 (ebk)
ISBN: 978-1-032-77097-0 (pbk)

Book DOI 10.4324/9781003481232

THE PSYCHOLOGY OF GOLF

BY
LESLIE SCHON

METHUEN & CO. LTD.
36 ESSEX STREET, W.C.
LONDON

First Published in 1922

CONTENTS

CHAP.		PAGE
I	THE PSYCHOLOGY OF A SHORT PUTT	1
II	A RECIPE FOR PERFECTION	9
III	THE EYE AND THE BALL	17
IV	THE HABIT OF THE SWING	27
V	MENTAL CONCENTRATION AND GOLF'S LITTLE WORRIES	34
VI	THE GOLFING TEMPERAMENT	41
VII	THE CONFESSION BOOK	49
VIII	PUTTING AND AUTO-SUGGESTION	57
IX	THE LURE OF LONG DRIVING	66
X	"JUST NOT" SHOTS	73
XI	A VINDICATION OF THE THEORIST	79
XII	A PHILOSOPHY FOR BUNKERS	85
XIII	GOLF IN A GALE	91
XIV	THE PSYCHOLOGY OF MATCH PLAY	97
XV	THE PSYCHOLOGY OF MATCH PLAY (*concluded*)	106
XVI	CONCLUSION	114
	INDEX	119

THE PSYCHOLOGY OF GOLF

CHAPTER I

THE PSYCHOLOGY OF A SHORT PUTT

"The greatest and most commanding of all the wonders of life is unquestionably the mind of man."—*Haeckel*

LOOKING back, after two years of probing into the mystery of the mind and the part that it plays in golf, it seems to me somewhat absurd that any golfer should need to be convinced of the vital bearing of the mind on the game he plays. Yet whenever I have cornered any stranger at my home club, and have hurled my theories at him, invariably have I found him ignorant of what, to me, appears an obvious fact: that the mental side of the game is vastly more important than the physical side.

Golfers seem to have accepted as a mystery the uncertainty of golf. They have played badly when they have felt physically fit, and they have golfed well when they have felt exceedingly ill. Indeed, a friend of mine, a doctor of medicine, has told me that he played the round of his life when feeling very ill; actually he took his temperature on the eighteenth green and found it to be 101.

Naturally many players have wondered why such things should be, and yet I have never discovered one who, to my way of thinking, has lighted on the

THE PSYCHOLOGY OF GOLF

answer to the riddle. But surely that answer must be contained in the simple little word of four letters, the *Mind*.

Courteous Reader, you must picture me as a kind of Don Quixote, a tilter at windmills, for I myself think that I am like a man who has discovered a gold mine under the Bank of England. Can I convince the Directors of that august Bank of the desirability of pulling down the building and sinking a shaft ? Can I convince you, Courteous Reader, that for all the years golf has been played, golfers have been knocking their feather balls, or their gutties, their floaters, or that modern atrocity the rubber-cored ball, over the tops of numberless gold mines ? or in other words, that since the beginning of the game, golfers have studied the comparatively unimportant physical side and have never heeded the vitally important mental side ?

Such has been the case in other matters as important as golf. In education, for example, teachers have been prattling of training the child's mind without having even an ephemeral knowledge of psychology. The truth of this you must grant me, although you may be surprised that I class a game, such as golf, as equally important with a vital national matter, such as education. But it is not my business, or at any rate my desire, to explain the greatness of golf. I am making an attempt to help the average golfer improve his game, nothing more.

I think the beginner at golf affords a remarkable example of the mental side of the game. You tee up a ball for him and give him a driver, and more often than not he manages to hit the ball somewhere on the face of the club. Often he sends the ball quite

THE PSYCHOLOGY OF A SHORT PUTT

a long way, straight as an arrow. This is a notorious fact, and if you allow the beginner to play a whole round, keeping his score for him, he usually plays some twenty strokes above the average novice's form. That is, if he takes up the game it will be six or possibly twelve months before he equals his first round. Why? Simply because his friends don't give him a chance. They tell him that he must get worse before he gets better; that golf is a terrifically difficult game, and that his first round was a series of flukes and miracles, that cannot by any possible chance, or combination of chances, be repeated. What utter nonsense!

After all, what is there in this game of golf? You have simply got to learn to swing with a wooden club, to hit your iron shots, to putt, and to learn to judge the effect of the wind on the flight and run of your ball, and beyond that, nothing. If we except the few objectionable tags—one cannot dignify them by the title axioms — "Keep yer e' a' the ba'," "Never up, never in," and "A match is not lost until it is won."

This is the physical side of the game, the A B C. Anyone with average intelligence, provided he gives his mind to the task, and has plenty of spare time, can master this A B C in six months or a year. Indeed there are hundreds of golfers who have mastered this A B C, they can drive straight and for a reasonable distance, play their iron shots crisply, pitch accurately and putt steadily, but their handicaps are six or seven simply and solely because they have not learnt the mental side of golf. Their rounds are made up of perfect golf sandwiched between vile golf. Every three or four holes they have a lapse, foozle a drive or top an iron shot, because they have lost control of their minds. Can there be any other explanation that fits the facts ? I think not!

As says Dr. Watts: "The mind's the standard of the man." Here let me cut my preamble short, and let us study the mind of the golfer through the medium of the short putt.

First, let us ponder over the difference in mental attitude between the average golfer and the expert, and lord! what a difference there is. Your sixteen-handicap man will swagger up to the ball and knock it into the hole contemptuously ; the expert sidles up to his ball, in the hope, I imagine, of catching it unawares, and he will take great pains over the putt. And does the expert hole a much higher percentage of short putts ? I think not. Again, how easy it is to knock the ball into the hole from a yard away when one's opponent has picked up, and why the deuce can't one knock one's putts into the hole in this fashion in a Medal round ? Obviously the reason why many golfers cannot be sufficiently carefully careless is because their mind needs to be trained. They insist upon realizing the difficulties when their motto ought to be "Don't realize the difficulties and then there won't be any ! "

This fear of short putts ought to be classified among the numerous diseases of the brain; the fear of open spaces and the fear of crowds are both well known to the medical profession. Yardputtophobia is, I think, a suitable name for the disease.

Most golfers when they are searching for the reason, or reasons, for a missed yard putt, do not look beyond their nose ; they do not realize that the actual cause is more often than not entirely disconnected from the

THE PSYCHOLOGY OF A SHORT PUTT 5

actual putt. For instance, a player may be short with a putt on the eighteenth green, and in consequence he may lose his match. Undoubtedly this failure will rankle, and in his next round, which may be a week later, he will suddenly remember this putt with the result that he will putt wildly past the hole. This is an extreme instance, although I feel certain that every golfer will remember a bad shot at a certain hole when next he plays that hole. But whether this is so or not, it is certain, to my mind, that any short putt is simply a link in a chain. If you have ever noticed a train starting from a station you will have seen the chains which connect carriage with carriage gradually tighten, and you must consider a putt like these gradually tightening chains. The centre link is influenced by the links in front of it, and in turn it influences the links behind.

One incident which happened on my home course many months ago, and which has remained fresh in my memory, illustrates this point. The green at the first hole is guarded by a water hazard some six feet in depth. I had been outdriven from the tee, but had played my second shot to within a foot of the pin; actually my ball appeared to be almost in the hole, or rather resting against the flag. My opponent topped his second shot, and as his ball raced along the baked fairway, I muttered to myself " One up ! "—but to my surprise my opponent's ball ran through the hazard. Thus I had first of all been filled with joy, this had turned to surprised disgust, and this in its turn became changed to annoyance when I found my ball was over a yard short of the hole. Doubtless you can fill in the remainder of the picture for yourself. My opponent holed his putt, and I missed mine!

In the course of a match it is very difficult to avoid speculating on the result of each hole after the tee shots have been played, but a player must realize that there is an unknown factor—the play of one's opponent—that cannot be estimated but which should never be overlooked. Surely the average golfer does not realize the dangers of this speculating, for, let his opponent lay an approach dead and down comes the aerial castle, over goes the apple cart. But worse still, the player's confidence is shaken, the castle must be rebuilt, and the apples picked up.

This speculating is, to my mind, the most important mental process as regards putting, but it hinders a player without helping him in the slightest. Naturally, it is not the only mental process. Even before a player steps on to a green he commences collecting data, or perhaps it would be more correct to say reviewing data, that will help him when he comes to putt. Again this seems to me to be a dangerous practice; true, if the fairway is wet, it is logical to assume that the green will be wet and thus slow, but in these days of scientific drainage and of plateau greens, it is folly to speculate on the pace of the green until you actually reach it. Once on the green, then your sense of touch, even through a stout-soled shoe, will tell you a great deal unless you neglect the evidence. Your sight will tell you as much more: the grass may be long and badly need cutting. And beyond this your memory will tell you a lot of things, possibly many of them will be inconvenient things, best forgotten: that you hooked your last putt on this particular green, or pushed it. Indeed, I am almost certain that

THE PSYCHOLOGY OF A SHORT PUTT 7

golfers miss short putts solely through the treachery of their memory, which at the most awkward time possible reminds them of numberless other short putts that have somehow missed their mark.

Even in the examination of the "line" to the hole, the memory plays a great part, for it is obviously only by other examples that a golfer can calculate the correct allowance for a slope. But again, he must remember putts that have correctly allowed for the slope of the ground, or his putting will lack confidence at a critical moment.

Finding the correct line to the hole and calculating the required strength is, if we can believe James Sherlock, as easy as repeating the five-times table. He assures us that the difficult part of putting is to hit the ball on the right line with the required strength. Well, there is no mystery about the swing of a club. It is done through the contraction of certain muscles by a discharge of nerve force which passes from the brain down the nerve fibres which connect with all our muscles. There is no conjuring trick in the matter. A cow, for instance, walks on its four hoofs by a similar process. Thus the player concentrates on the ball, makes up his mind as to what he wants to do, and it is his will-power that sets the delicate mechanism at work. Back goes the putter, down it comes, and away goes the ball, whether into the hole or not hardly matters at the moment, for it is the registration of the result that is of paramount importance. And here, I must repeat again, lies one of the secrets of good putting. A good putt is speedily forgotten; a bad putt lingers in the memory. This, of course, is not true of every putt. If you hole out from the edge of the last green in a critical match, doubtless you remember it for a long time; but if a golfer holes a similar putt in the early stages of the game he usually walks off the green immediately, as much as to say: "Come on, my friend, your half-crown is mine, and I'll have it as soon as possible." And an impression that is not a vivid one is soon forgotten, if, indeed, it is registered in the brain at all.

But a bad putt! We at once want to know the cause of our failure; regardless of the crush behind, we desire to try it again. This is all very well in its way, but a match is not the time for eradicating mistakes. Besides which, the wisdom of such a proceeding is doubtful. Suppose we miss the putt again and again, the effect on our play is likely to be bad, for our memory will drag that wretched little putt before us when we are faced with a critical "yarded" to win the match.

CHAPTER II

A RECIPE FOR PERFECTION

WHETHER a stroke in golf is a short putt, a full "bang" with a wooden club, an iron shot of a hundred and fifty yards, or a clip shot of half that distance, the underlying principles must be the same if it is to be played perfectly.

Firstly, there must be the collection of all the factors effecting the shot: the distance to the hole; the condition of the turf; the strength and direction of the wind. These must be weighed up and balanced against every similar successful stroke that our memory can conjure up.

Secondly, having decided to use a mid-iron and to play a half-shot with it, pitching the ball on a certain piece of the fairway, there is the actual playing of the stroke.

Finally, there is the registering of the result for future use.

"Good heavens!" I can hear you cry, Courteous Reader, "there is nothing new in this. It is simply a roundabout way of saying that a golfer considers what kind of shot he is going to play, then plays it, and just watches what happens."

True enough! that is what the average golfer does, but the trouble is he does several other things besides. The mental attitude of the average golfer reduces him to a kind of " doubting Thomas " state. He lacks belief in himself, he doubts his own powers. Although he knows that he ought to use, let us say, a brassie, he doesn't like the lie, he doesn't think he can pick up the ball when it is lying so close. So he takes a mid-iron and presses, with the inevitable result.

Thus at the very outset he commits the very worst possible fault. He is clear about what he wants to do, but he is absolutely certain that he cannot do it. It is " with malice aforethought " that he takes the wrong club. Pray do not imagine that I am urging the novice or long-handicap player to use a brassie when his ball is buried; I am simply asking him not to funk using a wooden club when there is a very fair chance that a successful shot can be made with it. And when he is really sure that it is impossible to use a wooden club, I suggest that he considers exactly how far he can send the ball with an iron club without straining himself, and that he selects a spot which will simplify the approach to the hole and then plays an easy shot to this spot.

As a matter of fact, and not of fancy, this selection of the right club is of vital importance because the player who is not sure about what he wants to do is courting disaster. As Mark Twain would express it, he is " monkeying with a buzz-saw."

If there is any single recipe that will improve the average golfer's play, it is that he shall be absolutely sure about what he wants to do, and being sure he must imagine himself successful. This, I hold, is one of the essentials to good golf. It is, Courteous Reader, so terrifically important that I should like to repeat it, I should like to shout it in your ear,

A RECIPE FOR PERFECTION 11

only I know that you would be like the man in the poem, of whom it is written :

> "But he was very stiff and proud,
> He said, you need not shout so loud."

So I must content myself with quoting Dr. Wingfield-Stratford, who says this in his book, "The Reconstruction of Mind," "Ordinarily, whenever we decide on one course of action, other tendencies of the mind are like little cords or brakes, too feeble to stop the action altogether, but strong enough, though unperceived, to take off its edge, to weaken it to an indefinable extent. If we could only master the secret of performing our actions with absolute singleness of purpose, of knowing exactly what we want to do before we set out to do it, we should be not far off from being super-men." And I might add super-golfers!

Singleness of purpose! that must be our attitude towards every stroke we play. True, it cannot be acquired as easily as a new driver, but acquired it must be, even in a small degree, if a player hopes to make any real progress in the game. This surely explains why Braid, Taylor, and Vardon dominated the world of golf for so many years.

If you watch an average golfer, particularly when he is faced with a difficult shot, there is more often than not an extraordinary lack of purpose about his methods. He hesitates over the choice of a club, knows full well that he ought to use a mid-iron, flirts with this for a moment, only to replace it in his bag, and ultimately uses a mashie knowing that he is certain to "pull the ball round his neck!"

Of course, you, Courteous Reader, and I, know very

well that hesitation is fatal; as the adage has it, "He who hesitates is lost." But there is a vast difference between taking a little longer to make up one's mind and hesitating, which, so far as golf is concerned, implies a kind of "Dilly Dally" policy. Although every textbook on the physical side of golf deals at length with the fatal consequences of hesitating, I think that the sin is a venial one, or that it is not by any means difficult to overcome. It is simply a question of a little common sense.

On my home course there is a very cute little dog-leg hole which puts a premium on a long drive. There is no subtlety about the tee shot, no spectacular "carry" by means of which a corner can be cut off; the hole demands a plain, straight tee shot followed by an accurate second shot. The green is guarded by a deep hollow, and if your drive is neither long nor accurate, your only hope of a four lies in playing short and trusting to a good run-up to leave your ball dead. If I am playing with a man who is not a long driver, I always watch him closely at this hole, and I must confess that nearly every one of the short drivers hesitates over the second shot, and not only hesitates but goes for the million-to-one carry, and, further, the same players will attempt the same second stroke round after round. Obviously, in a golfing sense, experience doesn't teach fools to be wise; and so far as this dog-leg hole is concerned, once bunkered is not twice shy!

Learned men tell us that the rind of the brain is made up of millions of cells, but, at the age of thirty-five or thereabouts, these cortical cells are all full of impressions. It is, however, not a case of standing room only, we can discard an old impression to make

A RECIPE FOR PERFECTION

room for a new one—as a matter of fact, we do so every day. Hence there is no limit to the number of good strokes that a golfer can record. But they must be recorded methodically; they must be correctly labelled and put away into the right place, or it will be impossible to produce them when they are wanted. Take a simple instance : What is a wolf? Of course everybody knows what a wolf is, but very few people can give a concise definition. A wolf is an erect-eared, straight-tailed, harsh-furred, tawny-grey, wild, gregarious, carnivorous quadruped allied to the dog, etc., etc. Doubtless if you cornered an average man you could in time extract all this information from him. He would begin by telling you a wolf was carnivorous, then he would rake round in his mind and tell you that it was grey in colour and harsh-furred. If you asked him if that was all he could tell you, he would most probably reply " Yes," and yet, having started his mind to work, he would recollect, possibly a week later, that a wolf had erect ears. This may seem to have little connexion with the Royal and Ancient game, and I have no wish to extend the theme and bore you. But in a close match experience is the thing that counts, in fact in ninety-nine games out of a hundred which end on the last green it is the experienced player that wins. And after all, experience at golf simply consists of remembering the result of many strokes, and of having this data at hand when it is wanted. One often meets golfers who have reduced their handicap to a single figure after two or three years' play. Their long-handicap brethren speak of these golfers with bated breath, as if there was something magical in the process. Really there is no Black Art here. These players have gained experience quickly because they are able to make the best use of their minds. This is a matter that I must deal with later on.

I imagine that every player knows the reason why hesitation is fatal, there is proof of the fact in nearly every round the average golfer plays. Premonition of failure spells failure. If your opponent tops a tee shot at the critical stage in a game, and you say to him jestingly, possibly thetically: "P'raps I shall top too," as sure as bunkers are bunkers you will!

But if premonition of failure spells failure, the reverse also holds true; if you think you are going to succeed you are more than likely to. It is a source of surprise to most golfers that they can swing beautifully with their drivers when there is no ball to be hit, that they can drive half a dozen "screamers" down the middle of the fairway when there is no opponent, and they are practising after tea. Surely there is no mystery about this; it is the change in mental attitude that makes all the difference. It matters not at all if they top shot after shot, it is just like knocking a yard putt into the hole with the back of your putter when your opponent has picked up. But it is useless to try acquiring the "it doesn't matter" attitude when you play a match, because it does matter quite a lot.

The mental attitude that must be acquired is one of confidence in your own power, and I must confess that the simplest way to acquire and to hold this attitude is to have a practice swing before every shot. I am aware that this is a dangerous teaching because many golfers carry this practice-swing method to an extreme. They become a nuisance to other

A RECIPE FOR PERFECTION

players, holding up the course. But there is no need to waste time over the swing. Select your club, decide on the length of the shot you are going to play, say to yourself, This is what I am going to do (meaning, of course, when you make the actual stroke), have your practice swing, move straight up to your ball, and without any further consideration play the stroke. Here your imagination comes into play. The value of a vivid imagination in golf has, I think, never been fully realized. In a little book on " Golf Architecture," Dr. Mackenzie makes this truly astounding remark: " Every one knows how fatal imagination is in playing the game. Let the fear of socketting once enter your head, and you promptly socket every shot afterwards."

Frankly, this remark is absurd. Had the word uncontrolled been placed in front of the word "imagination," matters would have been entirely different. Dr. Mackenzie is a living proof of the fact that one can be a moderate golfer and a first-class golf-architect, but he must really be more careful in what he says about playing the game. The name of George Duncan will at once occur to every student of the game to disprove the Doctor's statement. Duncan's greatest trouble has been in controlling his imagination, but when he has it well under control there are few players who can keep up with the pace he sets.

If there is a Royal Road to good golf, it lies in controlling the imagination; instead of permitting it to be a hindrance and to suggest that you are likely to fail in a stroke, make it your servant. Imagine yourself succeeding, and you will succeed.

This is not an easy matter, the miracle cannot be performed in a night, and, like everything in this world worth having, it is the joy of the struggle and not the achievement that gives the keenest pleasure.

Why remain one of the "I knew I was going to top it" school of golfers?

CHAPTER III

THE EYE AND THE BALL

IT matters not a jot how grotesquely you grip your club, how abnormal is your stance, or how fantastic your swing, if you can keep your eye firmly on the ball for every shot you play you can reduce your handicap to a very low figure. Further, if your grip is moderately correct, if your stance is conducive to balance during a stroke, and if your swing possesses any rhythm, and you are good at keeping your eye on your ball, your handicap will come tumbling down to scratch.

There is not the slightest doubt about this, "no possible, probable shadow of doubt, no possible doubt whatever!"

If an examination is made of the methods used by writers of tales of mystery, it will be found that they one and all plunge their reader into the middle of the mystery in the first chapter. Sometimes they murder some unfortunate victim in the opening paragraph of the book. The psychology of attention is a remarkably interesting study, and the astute weaver of mysteries has sufficient acquaintance with the subject to know that he must catch and hold the reader's attention as soon as possible. The mystery of the Eye and the Ball is a unique parallel.

Among my golfing acquaintances I number several

who violate every known law of the game. Their grip and stance are fearfully wonderful ; their swing would make an angel weep, resembling a butcher chopping up a joint with a hatchet. But their handicaps are low because they have trained themselves to keep their heads down and their eyes on the ball.

When one comes to consider the matter in a philosophic manner, there is something extraordinarily funny in the fact that the average golfer cannot keep his eye on the ball. Indeed, the harder he tries, the more difficult it becomes.

For the past year I have attempted to arrive at an estimate of the number of times all classes of golfers take their eyes off the ball in an average round. Without having any definite proof, I think the eighteen-handicap player takes his eye off the ball about thirty-six times in each round, a twelve-handicap man about a dozen times, down to the scratch golfer, who probably lifts his head two or three times in eighteen holes. It is difficult to generalize about plus players, but they are by no means free from the disease. In their case the result is hardly noticeable to a long-handicap man ; the stroke is simply not quite so firmly or so accurately played.

But why on earth should it be difficult to keep one's eye on the ball ? It would seem the easiest thing possible to hit a stationary ball teed up on a pillar of sand.

"From a biological point of view, it is clear that attention must bear some direct relation to the needs of the organism. We attend to certain things primarily because they are, in one fashion or another, essential to our well-being. We are not always conscious of these needs ; one, for instance, may attend to a flash

THE EYE AND THE BALL

of light, or to a sharp pain, or to a moving object, for no conscious reason save that the stimulus, as we say, ' catches the attention.' But why are we so constituted that we attend to these things ? The real reason must be sought in race history. When our ancestors lived under very primitive conditions, as they did for thousands of generations, it was absolutely necessary for the existence of the organism that it be able to note any marked disturbance in its environment. Survival under primitive conditions was conditioned absolutely upon the instinctive tendencies to attend to all stimuli that could in any marked degree become danger signals." [1]

There is the solution, and quite an obvious one, to the riddle of the Eye and the Ball. You must remain motionless on the tee when your opponent is driving, so that you will not create a marked disturbance in his environment.

A moving ball, whether at cricket, tennis, or football, or indeed in any ball game, supplies the marked disturbance. True we may be beaten by the break or the swerve, but we try with all our will-power to watch the ball, because we cannot help doing so. Its movement provides the stimulus to our attention, and the remark of the golfing cricketer, that he was certain that he could hit the beastly little ball if his caddie was allowed to bowl it at him, is founded on the rock of fact. Have you ever heard of a cricketer taking his eye off the ball ? Of course not ; he can't if he wants to.

If the history of Homo Sapiens is traced back through the mists of ages, we find that our ancestors survived

[1] W. G. Bagley.

solely through their adaptability and versatility. If a cave-dweller forgot just once to attend to a marked disturbance, the brontosaurus got him.

Thus movement stimulates our attention, and the motionless little white golf ball does not.

Curiously enough, although every golfer knows that if he keeps his head down and his eye on the ball, the ensuing stroke is more than likely to be successful, this knowledge in itself is not sufficient stimulus. Obviously something stronger is needed, and, though it is not so obvious, I am convinced that it is the player's mental attitude that is wrong, and I am also convinced that that venerable maxim *Keep yer e' a' the ba' and dinna press*, is to blame. It is without doubt the worst possible phrase for conveying a particular meaning that could possibly be coined.

It is, I grant you, suitable for a phlegmatic Scot, but for the more highly strung Anglo-Saxon it is a vilely misleading phrase. A golfer needs an alert mental attitude towards his ball, he has got to concentrate for all he is worth. The sloppy frame of mind that this phrase engenders is useless. *Glare at the ball and smite it!*

That bright colours attract the attention is a fact well-known to psychologists, and while I was thinking over this problem of the Eye and the Ball, it occurred to me to try a painted golf ball. So I experimented with a "jazz" ball, and wrote a short article about it, which was printed in the *Daily Mail*.

Some slight interest was taken in the Press, and the criticism of the Golfing Correspondent of the *Evening News* raises a point of peculiar interest. Let me quote him in full:—

THE EYE AND THE BALL

"JAZZ" GOLF BALLS

"TIME THE HIT" IS THE RULE THAT COUNTS; IGNORE FADS AND FANCIES

The suggestion that a golf ball should be painted in Jazz colours to assist the player to keep his eye on it seems rather far-fetched.

The fact is that failure to hit the ball properly is all due to bad timing of the club.

If the blow be well and truly aimed the eye takes little part in the ultimate result.

A far better rule than "Keep your eye on the ball" is "Time the blow."

Now to be able to time a blow at will one must know how it is done, and that is precisely what the average golfer does not know. I have asked at least a dozen golfers how they timed a drive. One of them replied that he hadn't the faintest idea, but would be exceedingly obliged if I could tell him, and the remainder confessed that they didn't know how it was done, all they knew was that sometimes they timed their strokes, and at other times they didn't! So clearly the advice "Time the blow" will not assist us.

But the suggestion that if the blow be well aimed the eye takes little part in the ultimate result is very interesting—if it happens to be true. It raises the novel point, at what part of the swing does the golfer take his eye off the ball ?

Personally, my experiments cause me to think that the head is moved and the eye taken off the ball at the turning point in the swing, that is, when the club starts to come down, or possibly just before. This is in the majority of cases, but one sometimes sees the head lifted before the club reaches the top of the swing. In fact I was conscious of taking my eye off the ball in a round played a few days ago, long before the club had reached the top, and the ball, although it went peculiarly crooked, travelled a considerable distance. In the opinion of two experienced teachers of golf the novice usually takes his eye off the ball in the down swing.

It is my belief that if the eye is taken off the ball during any part of the swing, of course with the exception of the follow-through, control of the club is lost. In the case of the novice this lifting of the head is followed by a lifting of the whole body; the delicate balance of weight is lost, and with it the rhythm of the swing.

"Keep your eye on the ball in golf is a familiar statement of the fact that the movement of the arms is controlled immediately by attention to some object in the field of vision."

It seems to me that Mr. Pillsbury puts the matter in a nut-shell.[1] It is of course possible to argue that a professional can drive a golf ball when blindfolded, but this book is not intended as an aid to professional golfers! And doubtless it has fallen to the lot of every player to have his ball roll off the tee just as the club was descending and yet make a good drive. Surely this proves that the eye, or rather the brain through the agency of the eye, controls the club.

But at present we are far from having solved the *bête noir* of all beginners at golf, and unfortunately there is no magic secret the knowledge of which will compel us to glare at our balls for the remainder of our golfing lives.

[1] "Attention," W. B. Pillsbury. Sonnenschein.

THE EYE AND THE BALL

Attention cannot become a habit. The psychologists tell us that habit and attention are two extremes of mental life. We can habitually assume the attitude of attention, but I cannot see that this helps us very much. They are dull fellows, these psychologists!

Yet one of them gives us a ray of hope. He says : " There are many tasks that are not intrinsically interesting. Sometimes, however, after effort has been initiated and sustained by a powerful incentive, the task gradually becomes fascinating in itself. The incentive may now very well be forgotten, for its utility is at an end."

From a psychological standpoint the golfer must keep his eye on the ball throughout the whole stroke, until his arms and his body drag his head out of position. It is an extraordinarily dangerous teaching to say that the head should be lifted as soon as the club and ball part company, and that if this is not done the swing becomes cramped. For the golfer who is going to attempt any such thing must visualize himself lifting his head before he commences to swing. That way madness lies !

There is a simple little head-and-ball practice that is, I think, novel, and that has improved my own game wonderfully. It consists of playing chip shots without watching either the flight or the run of the ball.

Not more than six balls should be used, and they should be dropped, in the rough for choice, as close to the edge of a bunker as possible. The practice consists of chipping the balls over the bunker on to the green. This is a type of stroke that seems fatal to most beginners; it always makes them lift their head.

Actually the practice is absurdly difficult. For the

first two or three strokes it is easy, although the desire to watch the run of the ball when it pitches with a thud on the green is very great, but at the fourth or fifth attempt up comes the head. This is lack of concentration and nothing else; for although the stroke may be a good one, the player has failed in the attempt to keep his head down. An added incentive lies in putting out with the six balls, again not watching the run of any ball, and of keeping a record of the number of strokes taken.

In these days when many golfers find it difficult to get as much practice as before the war, and when, in consequence, they are often badly off their game, this practice will be found to be a kind of general golfing tonic, and a very excellent one. In a golfing sense it will cure nearly all the ills of the flesh. For instance, a player may suddenly develop a violent slice. Well-meaning friends will assure him that he is drawing his arms in; probably in the course of a single round they will tell him this a dozen times, until his patience is exhausted, and he snarls: " I know that ! But how the deuce am I to stop it ? "

In a case such as this it is the player's mind that is at fault; his arms don't draw themselves in out of pure cussedness, and I am sure that if he takes his mashie niblick and spends ten minutes over the eye-and-ball practice his trouble is more than likely to vanish. Before he plays each stroke he should visualize himself letting his arms go through freely after the ball. On the other hand, when used as a cure for topping, the player must imagine himself keeping his head as steady as a rock.

In reading through what I have written about the eye and the ball, an idea occurs to me that may be

THE EYE AND THE BALL 25

of interest to many golfers, and, to a few, of some practical value.

Psychologists tell us that there are many degrees of attention: when one is attracted by bright colours the attention is *passive*; but when, attracted by the colour, one becomes interested in the object itself, the attention passes into the *secondary passive form*. But so far as golfers are concerned, the classification of the Professor of Education in the University of London (Professor John Adams), seems to cover the case. Professor Adams divides attention into two forms: spontaneous attention, and voluntary attention. In those things that we attend to naturally, and without effort, our attention is spontaneous. Voluntary attention implies an effort of will, and is thus a higher form than spontaneous. In using this classification, let me say that Professor Adams has adopted this simplification to illustrate a point, and it must not be used " as evidence against him."

A simple experiment will prove that even those with the strongest will-power cannot concentrate their attention for more than a few seconds, and thus it would seem that there are two courses open to the golfer: he can take up his stance, waggle, and swing, while his attention is still voluntary, or, if he is very deliberate in these preliminaries, he can change his attention from voluntary to spontaneous. This is a proof, if proof was needed, of the soundness of the methods of George Duncan; he gets the whole business over while his attention is still in the higher form. Duncan's temperament is such that the progress from impression to action is exceedingly rapid, and thus to concentrate on his ball by voluntary attention, to waggle until his interest was aroused, and his attention changed to spontaneous, would be running counter to his temperament.

At times it seems impossible to focus the attention, and the golfer hits his ball when his attention is diffused. This is because there are beats of attention, a regular rise and fall between concentration and diffusion.

Surely even the experienced player should try to study his own peculiarities, and it might be well worth his while giving Duncan's rapid method an extended trial.

CHAPTER IV

THE HABIT OF THE SWING

I WONDER how many golfers realize that the swing of a golf club is just as much a habit as smoking, drinking a glass of port after lunch, or parting one's hair on the right, or left, of one's head. A habit is a very easy thing to acquire; and a very difficult thing to eradicate when once it has been acquired.

The head of a golf club during a full swing passes through a path nearly thirty feet in length, depending very much on the length of the club and the height of the player. During the swing numberless muscles come into play, and these muscles are contracted and relaxed in a regular order. One may liken a golfing swing to the movements of a conjurer, juggling with three billiard balls; often the conjurer will carry on an animated conversation with his audience while he is tossing the balls about, simply because long practice has made the movements that he performs into a habit.

In the chapter on "The Principle of Serviceable Associated Habits," in the "Expression of Emotions in Man and Animals," Charles Darwin says: "It is notorious how powerful is the force of habit. The most complex and difficult movements can in time be performed without the least effort or consciousness."

28   THE PSYCHOLOGY OF GOLF

It is not positively known how it comes that habit is so efficient in facilitating complex movements; but physiologists admit " that the conducting power of the nerve fibres increases with the frequency of their excitement."

Suppose a river runs across a sandy beach: the longer it runs the deeper will it cut its bed in the sand, and the less likely will it be to change its course. In much the same way the complex golfing swing becomes fixed as a habit and the more difficult does it become for a golfer to alter it. Manifestly, it is just as easy to acquire a good swing as a bad one, and the beginner, or the novice, who has a bad swing must put himself into the hands of his professional. Even the man who has been golfing for some years and who swings badly had better by far begin again : this remark applies to ninety players out of every hundred.

It is really extraordinary the number of golfers one meets with a very bad swing, players with quite low handicaps who spend hours in practising and more hours of thought, all absolutely wasted, because they are working on wrong lines. I am tempted to say, worse than wasted ; for these golfers are laboriously acquiring bad golfing habits.

"It is because the body is a machine that education is possible. Education is the formation of habits, the superinducing of an artificial organization upon the natural organization of the body ; so that acts, which first require a conscious effort, eventually become unconscious and mechanical." [1]

What the majority of golfers are doing is to

[1] Huxley.

THE HABIT OF THE SWING 29

superinduce bad habits on their natural organizations so that they may be performed mechanically ! It is somewhat funny, but at the same time extremely sad, to see the keenness with which many golfers practice when practice alone will not help them, when the fatal bar to further progress is knowledge, or rather, lack of knowledge. One often sees players with a pronounced pause at the top of their swing, not a Massy Twiddle, or an infinitesimal pause, but a pause of a second or more. Nearly all of these players are erratic drivers, and it is useless for them to go out and practise driving unless they go out determined to get rid of the habitual pause. But that is exactly what they do not do ; they seem to think that by driving ball after ball their length and accuracy will increase, and possibly they will, but only to an exceedingly small degree. Yet, if these golfers went out determined to eradicate the pause, there would be no limit to the improvement they might make.

So far as the average golfer is concerned, practice must be carried out with the definite object of forming new and good habits, and of eradicating bad habits, which is just the same thing, but differently expressed. And here, Courteous Reader, I can imagine you saying : " This is all very well. I know that if one's golf interferes with one's business, one must give it up, and although what you say about habits sounds true enough, I am a busy man. My only time for practice consists of a few half-hours each week. You can't expect me to give up my games, although I do want to improve my play."

Certainly I do not want you to give up your games, for the simple reason that if you practice properly half an hour at a time is quite long enough. To spend a whole afternoon in solemn practice would result in more harm than good, but I do suggest that your practice should be systematic, otherwise it will be valueless.

As an illustration of the eradication of a bad habit and the formation of a good habit, it seems to me to be very desirable to deal with slicing, which is the bugbear of almost all beginners.

Let us suppose that a novice is slicing all his tee shots. Firstly he must examine his driver, or get some one else to do so, for choice his local professional. If any doubt lingers in the mind of the novice that the fault may lie in the club, let him beg, borrow, or steal another. It will be fatal to carry on with the old one.

Satisfied with his driver, he must next consider what happens to a sliced ball when it is in the air. Here it seems better to state exactly what is meant by the term a sliced ball, for a drive that finishes in the rough on the right of the fairway is not necessarily sliced. A sliced drive is one that starts straight, or nearly straight, from the tee and curls in the air to the right of the line on which it started. The reason for this is that the ball is spinning from left to right, and the air pressure, being greater on the side which is turning into the wind, in this case the left side, pushes the ball to the right. A ball that is correctly driven, has back-spin imparted to it by the club, and obviously the air pressing on the underside of the ball tends to make it rise in its flight. A hooked ball naturally has the reverse spin to a sliced ball.

This is exceedingly elementary, but it is useful knowledge from a beginner's point of view, because

THE HABIT OF THE SWING 31

it may give him a clue as to why he is slicing. To impart a left-to-right spin to a ball, the face of the club must be drawn from right to left across the ball during the moment of impact. This right-to-left movement of the club may be the result of several faults : the player may be hitting at the ball, instead of through it, in other words, checking the swing of the club at a critical moment ; or the grip may be faulty, too tight with the left hand, too loose with the right, possibly the position of the hands on the shaft may be wrong ; or the player may be drawing in his arms and not throwing them, as it were, after the ball. Certainly the best method of locating the fault is to go to the professional, but failing him, most experienced golfers would be able to spot it.

But a fault that is located is by no means cured ; it is quite possible to know what you are doing wrong without being able to prevent yourself from continuing to do it—our old friend the force of habit again ; and thus we complete the circle and return to an earlier remark that the way to cure a bad habit is to contract a new and good one.

Occasionally a simple cure will overcome the slicing habit, such as turning the right hand a trifle more under the shaft or gripping a little tighter with it, or by taking up the normal stance and then drawing the right foot back a few inches. But in the beginner's case slicing is just like mumps or chicken-pox, one has got to have them in one's youth, and the golfing novice in every case has an attack, mild or severe, of slicing which more often than not wears itself out " without benefit of clergy." Personally I do not think that this attack of slicing is a necessary evil of golf, a part of the apprenticeship of the game, and

I feel convinced that if the novice takes it in hand it can be cured in a month or two instead of wearing itself out perhaps in the course of a year or even longer.

Once let the beginner satisfy himself that the fault does not lie in his club or his manner of gripping it, and the cure is easy enough. He selects a vacant tee and commences to superinduce his new habit. Taking up his stance about ten feet from the tin containing the sand, he must practise a few swings, attempting to hit the box. Naturally, this is impossible, and it is also impossible for the novice to draw in his arms, when trying to hit an object ten feet away. In making these swings care must be taken that the player's weight is not thrown forward on to his toes, but is kept well back on the heels, and before each swing the player must visualize himself letting his arms swing out freely after the imaginary ball is hit. There is no need to hurry over these swings, mind and muscles are very soon tired, and after half a dozen swings the player might tee up a ball. Not, I hope, with any great expectation of hitting it straight down the middle of the fairway; it is far more likely to be hit on the top. And this will supply the first acid test. The golfer who is annoyed because a habit has not been acquired in a few minutes, and who picks up his balls and walks home, will have to let his attack of slicing wear itself out. But the player who is not down-hearted will succeed.

Experts have laid down definite rules for the formation of habits, and I am certain that the two most important of these may be of use to golfers. First, the particular act or line of conduct must be kept within the focus of the attention; and second, there must be an avoidance of any exceptions.

THE HABIT OF THE SWING 33

In connexion with the latter, my own experience may be of interest. So strongly did I realize the value of always giving the hole a chance that I was at some pains to acquire the habit of being up with my approach putts. Certainly there were exceptions when I putted, or rather trickled the ball up to the hole simply to leave it " dead," but I made it a rule to be annoyed with myself, and this feeling of dissatisfaction had its effect. After two or three months I noticed a change in my putting: unconsciously I really was giving the hole a chance; and although this was some time ago, I think about eighteen months, the habit of being up seems permanent.

So far as my own experience goes, I do not think that the formation of a habit is very difficult so long as one keeps the resulting benefits firmly before one. The good habit of hitting through the ball and allowing the arms to go freely through will undoubtedly result in the novice's handicap being reduced from, say, eighteen to sixteen. Desire is a strong motive power.

To a very large extent the good golfer is simply a man who has formed a series of good golfing habits.

CHAPTER V

MENTAL CONCENTRATION AND GOLF'S LITTLE WORRIES

ONE often meets charming men, who, since they are unable to concentrate on the game unless players, caddies, and spectators are marshalled to their satisfaction, are a terrible nuisance on the links. These folk allow themselves to be annoyed by "golf's little worries."

"Would you mind standing a little more to the right? Thank you! Boy! Hi!! That caddy!!! How the dickens do you expect me to putt when you are dancing about behind me? Dash that woman in the white skirt! I honestly believe that she perches herself on the nearest hill for the sole purpose of catching my eye. Your wife? I'm *awfully* sorry, but really—you see?—er——don't you? ——"

After very careful consideration, I have used the words "allow themselves to be annoyed," for one frequently meets golfers who are not disturbed whatever you, your caddy, or casual onlookers may do. I remember playing in a three-ball on one occasion when a caddy dropped a bag of clubs just as one of the players was swinging down at the ball. The clubs dropped with a mighty rattle and crash, but it made no difference at all to the stroke, which was played perfectly.

MENTAL CONCENTRATION

As a matter of fact, and not of fancy, many players excuse themselves after a bad stroke by a—terminological inexactitude. Having foozled, they perceive a white skirt on the skyline, and then treat their opponent to a dissertation on such a subject as " Should women be allowed within a mile of a golf course ? "

They wax exceedingly indignant ; they swell with righteous wrath. Play-acting, very clever play-acting, so clever that they really do feel angry, and their golf suffers at the next two or three holes in consequence.

Now when a player is concentrating on a stroke he is in some respects mad ; for a second he is a monomaniac ; he is possessed with an *idée fixée;* his singleness of purpose is absolute if he is really concentrating. And I cannot for the life of me see how anything can disturb him unless he allows it to. If this does happen, then, in my opinion, he cannot be giving his whole mind to the stroke, he isn't concentrating.

Let me make a confession that will also illustrate my meaning with great clarity ; a day or two ago, in the course of a round, two peculiar incidents took place. On the seventh tee my opponent dropped his golf ball just as I was starting my club on the down swing. His ball fell about eighteen inches behind my ball and just out of the path of my club, and, much to my opponent's surprise, it made no difference to my tee shot. From this you might infer that as usual I topped my drive, but I didn't ; my ball went quite straight and a reasonable, if not extraordinary, distance. The second incident happened on the seventeenth tee : again I was just going to drive when, to vary the monotony, my opponent's caddy started walking very briskly towards the green. Here is my confession: I stopped in the middle of my swing and glared at the brute. Of course there wasn't the slightest need for me to do this, I could have hit my average drive without any trouble, but the caddy's action seemed not so much rude as insulting. He stepped off with a jaunty air, as much as to say: Golfers are harmless lunatics, designed by an all-wise Providence for putting easily earned money into *my* pocket; but this particular golfer is quite the worst player I have ever seen and really I can't be bothered to watch him. So you see it was my pride that he offended, and this, I feel certain, is the reason why numberless players are annoyed at any violation of the rules of etiquette. It is not their play that is likely to suffer, but their pride that will suffer.

But once a player gets into the habit of being put off his game by these little worries, he is unlikely to make any progress in the game, and he will wander round a course looking for things at which to be annoyed, actually seeking them. Few golfers realize that their game cannot stand still, whether their handicap is scratch, eight, or eighteen; their standard of play must either progress or retrogress, improve or deteriorate, according to the amount they play or practise.

In a previous chapter I have mentioned the rules, if they can be called rules, for concentration: that you must be clear about what you want to do first of all, and then you must imagine yourself doing it. So far as concentration at golf is concerned, this does not go quite far enough, and the interesting question arises, What should be the state or condition of a player's mind when he is actually making a stroke?

In connexion with this, Mr. George Greenwood,

MENTAL CONCENTRATION

in writing in the *Daily Telegraph* on the Oxford and Cambridge Golf Match, which has just been played at Princes, suggests the obliteration from the mind of a bunker that is directly in the line of play. I might say (but I have not any intention of doing so) that Mr. Greenwood has chosen the wrong word, and I might hazard the opinion that a correspondent who has to wire his article to a daily paper, probably in the deuce of a hurry, has very little time to choose his words. From my knowledge of Mr. Greenwood's articles, I know that he doesn't use the wrong word, and I know that it was " with malice aforethought " that he wrote that nasty word *obliterate*. My argument is this : Was the player who foozled into the bunker thinking of the bunker when he played his stroke, or did he imagine that it was quite likely that he would foozle into the bunker ?

By a law to which there are no exceptions, the will yields to the imagination. As an illustration of this, anyone can walk along a plank a foot in width when it is lying on solid earth; but place that plank across the two trestles of a bridge, twenty feet up in the air, and not one person in twenty will walk calmly across it, *because they imagine that they are likely to fall off*! Undoubtedly this player in the 'Varsity match actually imagined his ball hopping into the bunker, and that was his last conscious act before making the fatal stroke.

Can there be any other meaning to the word concentration, in a mental sense, than a focusing of the attention ? and further, can you focus your attention on such a thing as a golf ball ? I answer these questions with another question : Does not the golfer focus his attention, not on the ball itself, but on some action connected with the ball ?

I grant you that you can concentrate on a golf ball, on the size of it, on its marking, or on the dents you may have made in it, but no player wishes to do this in the middle of a close match. So that when a golfer is "concentrating on his ball," he is in reality concentrating on the stroke he is about to make. He is focusing his attention on the desire to put his ball as near the hole as possible; and can it be doubted that the average golfer starts concentrating on his second shot long before he reaches his ball? This appears to me to be a fatal policy. It is well enough for a man to plan his method of play for the whole of any particular hole when he is on the tee, and yet I do not think that even this is a good plan. You may hit your tee shot, "as per schedule," only to find that your ball is reposing in an old divot mark, and that it is thus quite impossible to use a brassie for your second shot. So the whole of your concentration is wasted.

The ideal method of playing golf is not to use your mind until you have to. When you reach your ball, then concentrate as hard as you can, for on your powers of concentration your next stroke depends. I have already drawn attention to the care which every player must exercise when selecting the club which he is going to use. I have said, in common with every other writer on the game, that hesitation is fatal, but it seems to me desirable that I should now amplify that statement. "He who hesitates is lost," because he isn't concentrating. If you concentrate hard enough you cannot hesitate, provided you are clear about what you are concentrating on.

Naturally every player has the desire to make the best shot that he possibly can, the trouble is that

MENTAL CONCENTRATION 39

the desire is not strong enough. This, I think, explains why it is so difficult to play pawky golf. So often a player has a lead of two or three holes, and, as says a stout golfer of my acquaintance, " he tries to sit on this lead, like an old hen on a setting of eggs." He attempts to hit his drives down the middle of the course, and to do so is content to sacrifice twenty yards in length, in playing his second shot he has no particular desire except that of avoiding trouble. In fact, his desire is of a negative kind, and in nearly every case he fails to achieve his end.

There still remains unanswered the question: " What is the state of a player's mind when he actually makes the stroke ? " and that is easily answered. Beyond the fact that he glows, as one glows on getting out of a cold bath, with a sense of pleasurable anticipation, his mind is a blank. Concentration by its very nature, precludes worry; if you concentrate on a stroke properly you cannot worry about the result.

Every stroke in golf represents a problem, but I fear that the average golfer neglects to make use of all the data. He, more often than not, attempts to hit his ball without making up his mind where he wants to hit it. It is not enough to try hitting your brassie shot at a long hole *in the direction of the green*, you must concentrate (I am heartily sick of repeating this word !) either on hitting your ball *on to the green*, or on to some *particular piece of the fairway*, from which the green can be easily approached.

It is just the same, only rather more so, in playing an iron shot. To get somewhere on to the green is not enough, you must concentrate on placing your ball near the pin, and to do this you must select the actual spot on the green, or possibly on the fairway, on which your ball must pitch so that at the end of its run it will be near the hole. This is a lesson that the inland golfer seldom learns. I imagine that hundreds of golfers work on the ridiculous theory that it is next to impossible to select a spot on which to pitch an iron shot; they argue that if they lift the ball fairly high in the air, it will carry a long way without much run, alternatively if they half top the shot, it will carry a short distance and run the rest of the way. Thus a shot played with a lot of run and a short carry, will equal the same stroke played with a lot of carry and a little run. On a seaside course, with a very undulating fairway, they will speedily be disillusioned, because it is necessary to calculate with considerable care exactly where your ball is going to pitch, whether on an uphill slope or a downhill slope, makes all the difference in the world.

As an elementary exercise in concentration, I would suggest that the novice takes a mid-iron and four or five balls to a hole that requires a stout iron shot after the tee shot. Beginning about eighty yards only from the green, he should select the spot on which he thinks his ball ought to pitch to run nicely up to the hole. Then, instead of playing a shot, he should walk up to this selected spot and place one of his spare balls on it. Now let him go back and play his remaining balls on to the green, concentrating on pitching his ball on the marked spot. After a dozen satisfactory strokes he can remove the marking ball, and try playing without its aid. Then if his strokes are still finishing on the green, he can increase the distance, finally moving to another hole and discarding the marking ball.

CHAPTER VI

THE GOLFING TEMPERAMENT

CONCERNING the golfing temperament, very much nonsense has been written. Personally, I have a very great liking for the idea of the ancients that a man was composed of the four elements, earth, air, fire and water. If one of these predominated it fixed the temperament of that particular man. Thus, four parts of air to one each of earth, fire and water, and you had a man mercurial in his actions and his ideas; ten parts of fire, a particularly hot-tempered fellow.

Nowadays we recognize two fundamental temperaments, the sanguine and the melancholic; the phlegmatic being but a degree of the sanguineous, the choleric of the melancholic. The nervous and the artistic temperaments are in the balance; some writers recognize them, others do not.

But pray do not attempt to determine which temperament any of your golfing friends may possess, for though, for our sins, we are all acquainted with the choleric temperament on the links, the temperaments merge so imperceptibly into one another that division into hard and fast classes is impossible. Moreover, golf seems to develop people's temperaments and certainly it intensifies them in an extraordinary manner. You may know a man for a score of years most intimately, but if he suddenly takes up golf you may find, nay, you will find, that twenty years of friendship has taught you very little of the real man. A sedate, solid, peace-loving business man may become transformed into a bloodthirsty, cave-dwelling barbarian just as quickly as it took James Braid to change from an average driver into a mighty long one. And that, in case you do not know, was one night.

But though it is impossible accurately to determine the temperament of any particular golfer, except in rare instances, and in the case of well-known players, there is no doubt, or very little, as to what constitutes the ideal golfing temperament.

To play good golf you must be sanguine of your own abilities, then you will be able to hit your best drives and hole three-foot putts as casually as you flick an inquisitive mosquito off your forehead. But while never doubting your own ability, you must never underrate that of your opponent. You must say to yourself: He's a good golfer, but I will beat him. And, of course, you must not be nervous; the greater the gallery the better your play must be; and when hordes of onlookers dance behind you as you attempt to play your tee shot, you must not be perturbed. . . . But, Courteous Reader, I am telling you what you already know, and what, doubtless, you do not wish to hear repeated. For most golfers are aware of defects in their temperament. They know that so far as they are concerned, one onlooker will make them nervous; two will cause them to top a high percentage of their shots; while a crowd makes them lose their head completely. So we come to the exceedingly interesting points: Can temperament be altered, and if it can, is it desirable to alter it?

THE GOLFING TEMPERAMENT 43

First of all let us consider what the word " temperament " really means. Says my Concise Oxford Dictionary : " Temperament is the individual character of one's physical organization permanently affecting the manner of thinking, feeling and acting."

In other words, it is our reaction to a stimulus, or on occasions, our lack of reaction to a stimulus, since I remember hearing of a man " so lethargic that no stimulus affects him." It is very curious how golfers react to different stimuli ; with some a good start to a medal round is fatal ; it is too great a strain to live up to the golf they have already played, and they permit their imagination to conceive a really bad hole. They calculate ahead, even selecting the hole at which they think they may waste a few strokes. Others are never happy unless they start with a brace of sixes, but once their partner has marked a six or two on their cards they are content. Now, they say to themselves, let us begin, and they finish their round in a blaze of glory. Although, more often than not, their bad start costs them the medal, they do not care in the least little bit. They accept as a fact, not that they must start badly, but that they cannot play good golf unless they do start badly.

It is usually in the last few holes of a close match that every golfer's temperament will make itself manifest ; some will play steadily on, others will play unexpectedly well, but the vast majority, to use a vulgar, if expressive phrase, will " fade away."

Study the matter as carefully as you like, and you will find that no man born of woman (this clause excludes Colonel Bogey), was ever gifted with an ideal golfing temperament as a kind of birthright. So the answer to the first of our conundrums : Can temperament be altered or modified ?—must be in the affirmative. I am aware that such a teaching will be opposed by many, yet to my mind there can be no doubt about it, and modern psychologists say very definitely, that a man's temperament is under his own control.

But the question : Is it desirable to modify one's temperament ?—raises a very debatable point, and so far as golf is concerned, no two writers seem in agreement. Here, I do not wish to use one of my pet phrases. I neither think, nor am I almost certain, neither dubious, nor doubtful, but as absolutely positive as one can be, that whether one likes it or not, golf will modify one's temperament. Indeed, I would go further, and say that a reduction in handicap of a golfer over 25 years old, is due more to a modification of temperament than to anything else. There comes a time in the life of every golfer when he, as it were, finds his feet ; when his improvement, which hitherto has been steady, reaches a vanishing point. Possibly it takes the average player some months to find this out ; some may never find it out at all. This is when the physical side attains a certain level, and is unable to proceed further unless attention is paid to the mental side of the game.

I might use the analogy of a boy leaving school to fend for himself in the world ; there are no text-books to assist him ; his success or his failure lies in his own hands. To succeed he must have confidence in himself, and confidence he is unlikely to acquire unless he examines his own thoughts and feelings, or in other words, becomes introspective.

One of the wonders of the mind is that it can be introverted upon itself ; it can be made to explain its workings ; and the golfer, like the schoolboy, must

THE GOLFING TEMPERAMENT 45

make a careful examination. At times the element of fire gains control of most golfers, and if there is one emotion that is a sure hindrance to improvement, it is loss of temper.

"We will turn to the characteristic symptoms of Rage. Under this powerful emotion, the action of the heart is much accelerated, or it may be much disturbed. The face reddens, or it becomes purple from the impeded return of the blood, or it may turn deadly pale. The respiration is laboured, the chest heaves and the dilated nostrils quiver. The whole body trembles. The voice is affected. The teeth are clenched or ground together, and the muscular system is commonly stimulated to violent, often frantic action. But the gestures of a man in this state differ from the purposeless writhings or struggles of one suffering from an agony of pain; for they represent, more or less plainly, the act of striking or fighting with an enemy."[1]

Ye Gods! What a word-painting of a choleric golfer who has missed a short putt. I think that every golfer has at times experienced the emotion of rage so vividly described by Charles Darwin. And rage, as I have already said, is fatal to good golf because it implies a loss of self-control. There are a number of amateur golfers on the border line that separates first class from second class players, who become peevish and throw their clubs about upon the slightest provocation. Some of these men do improve and are able to master their temper, and I think that they offer a proof that temperament must be modified.

There is no emotion that cannot be sublimated, or diverted into useful channels. There is really no need

[1] "The Expression of Emotions in Man and Animals." Darwin.

to throw one's clubs about, or to vent one's spite upon an innocent caddy. Bottle the energy up, as it were, and uncork it on the next tee. It may add twenty yards to one's drive! I write in all seriousness; though it may seem paradoxical to suggest that one should keep one's temper when one has lost it.

Speaking generally, it is the temperament of many golfers that makes it difficult for them to concentrate on a stroke at a critical stage in a match. At such a time some players, by no wide stretch of the imagination, might be termed temporarily insane. They do the wildest, most absurd things. Mr. Matthias Alexander would call this a "domination of conscious reasoned control by subconscious unreasoned desire."[1] It amounts to a loss of mental balance. Under these conditions the golfer is swayed by his animal instincts; instincts, for instance, which cause an ostrich to hide its head in the sand to escape pursuit, and which causes a level-headed golfer to take a mid-iron, when he knows that he cannot possibly reach the green unless he uses a brassie, just because he imagines he may hook or slice at a critical time when a bad shot may lose him the hole.

I have mentioned before how essential it is to control the imagination, but this is easier said than done; the ostrich has not sufficient brain to imagine that even with its head in the sand its body will be prominent, the golfer has the power of controlling his imagination, but such power needs to be developed. Unfortunately for themselves, there are thousands of golfers who "crack" badly in most close matches, and the problem that confronts these golfers is, firstly,

[1] "Man's Supreme Inheritance." Methuen.

THE GOLFING TEMPERAMENT 47

to find out what they do under such circumstances; and, secondly, why they do what they do. For, until a man knows himself, until he has at least a nodding acquaintance with his subconscious or hidden self, I do not see how he can make any real progress. Improve he may, but it will be a slow process, a groping in the dark.

Going to the other extreme in match play, one often meets golfers who play exceedingly well in a close game. Their drives fly straight and far; the hole appears magnetically to attract their second shots; and their putts rattle into the tin. This, at the psychological moment. The golf critics of the London newspapers tell us so often that such folk are superb match players that we have, many of us, come to agree with this view. For instance, in a recent important match Mr. T. lost four of the five five holes to Mr. P., and with our eggs and bacon the next morning, we were told that Mr. T. once again demonstrated what a wonderful match-player he is. But surely here is our old stimulus again. If anyone is going to try and convince me that Mr. T. requires to be three or four holes down before he can play his natural game, I am going to reply that herein lies the reason for the great gulf between professional and amateur golf, and that Mr. T's. temperament requires modification.

The man who plays good golf only when it is of paramount importance, is more often than not the man who plays slack, careless golf at the beginning of a round. He is like a racehorse that will not gallop unless whip and spur are used; and this is true of nearly every amateur golfer. With the professional it is a very different matter. He doesn't wait until he is three down and then make a supreme effort, neither does he "slack off" when he is two or three up; whatever lead he may gain, he attempts to add to. Bread and butter, too often bread without any butter, the bare necessities of life, that is the stimulus that makes the professional play good golf. Mr. Bernard Darwin has said that the professional knows very well that one bad shot begets another, and the average golfer might well adopt it as a motto. It reminds me of the jingle about big fleas and little fleas. For one bad shot begets another, several bad shots make up a bad round, one bad round leads to several bad rounds, "and so *ad infinitum.*"

Once a golfer discovers in what way his temperament is hindering his improvement, he will be well on the road towards good golf. I am tempted to wonder whether golfers as a body are as truthful as anglers; hundreds of them have assured me that they would do anything, or give anything, to improve their play. I fear that many of them imagine that there is some deep-hidden, simple, little secret which, when discovered, will effect some magic result. True there is such a secret—it is hidden in the words of Solon: "KNOW THYSELF."

CHAPTER VII

THE CONFESSION BOOK

IN writing of the muscular contractions by means of which a golf club is swung, I have attempted to make clear that such a movement becomes a habit performed subconsciously. But, besides his swing, nearly every golfer acquires a series of what might be termed "golfing habits," some of which may be of use, but others which certainly are not.

On an inland course where a player seldom has much wind to contend with, it is easy to get into the habit of playing each short hole with a particular club. Since the conditions do not often change, this club may be the right one for several months on end. Let us suppose that the short hole is 160 yards long, and that an easy shot with a mid-iron will put the ball on the green. If a stiff wind springs up, the obvious thing to do is to take a more powerful club and to play the stroke with the same easy swing. But does the average player do this? I am positive that he does not; he may consider the use of a heavier club; he may know quite well that he ought not to use his mid-iron, but he finds that he cannot make a change. He cannot imagine the stroke successfully played with any other club but that mid-iron, so he puts a little more power into the stroke, and the result is failure.

A habit once acquired sticks to a golfer as the Old Man of the Sea stuck to Sindbad, and yet with this vital difference. Sindbad was conscious of the weight of the old gentleman on his back and did his best to get rid of him, but the golfer is not conscious of the habit.

The subconscious mind has been described as a lumber-room; and the description is an apt one, for ideas, even beliefs, on all manner of subjects, ill-considered and ill-arranged, are stored in it. There is very little doubt—to my mind no doubt whatever—that in golf, a habit firmly rooted in a player's subconscious mind may cause him to act in a definite way, to the prejudice of his game, without his being aware of it. I have already explained that the way to get rid of a bad habit is to form a good one to take its place.

In a little book called "Mind Concentration," by Mr. K. T. Andersen, there is this extremely interesting remark: "Others," writes Mr. Andersen, "declare that they understand perfectly that a cessation of worry and 'fussing' is likely to have an improving effect on a person's general health and the amount of physical energy at his command, but they cannot believe that the need of and the desire for money is going to bring wealth, or that asking for freedom can in any way make them independent of the circumstances which have governed their lives for years past. . . . I would reply that it depends on *what* they want, *how much* they want it, and whether they are good at clearing out the storehouse of their subconscious minds where for years they have been treasuring a hundred thousand beliefs they have never tried to prove, and which they would find of no good

THE CONFESSION BOOK 51

if they did so, and filling it instead consciously with sound furniture. . . ."

And here, Courteous Reader, you may well exclaim: Here endeth the first lesson! and I can picture you turning languidly to another chapter, even flinging the book into a corner of the room. I might adopt the Shavian method of being rude to you, but instead I will propound a riddle : In what respects does a long handicap golfer resemble a criminal? Permit me to tell you the answer, since I am one of those persons who have a strong objection to riddles. Both are mentally incomplete. Hunger may drive a man to pick a pocket, and thus the golfer whose handicap remains at eighteen is the more incomplete of the two.

I have mentioned the instinct of self-preservation that causes the ostrich to hide its head in the sand, and although my golfing parallel may have been weak, our instincts do play an important part in the game. They graduate into reflex actions, into involuntary acts performed independently of our will. At times instinct and will struggle for the possession of our mind.

Surely every golfer has been confronted with the small, clear, Hyde-like voice of instinct. How often it has overcome the Jekyll within him. In my own case, it is with me at all times during a round, suggesting the most absurd things. That I shall take my brassie at the third hole when my ball is resting in a divot mark on a hanging lie, and when I know full well that it is beyond my powers to " pick the ball up," and that I gain very little if I do. At such a time, this little inward voice swells in volume, becomes very clamorous, very insistent, and extremely plausible. It thunders at me, if I show signs of yielding, as the wraith of the Cardinal thundered at Major the Honourable John William Wentworth Gore, when that sportsman of sportsmen tried to throw away a memorable match. " Ye fushionless eediot ! What's come ower ye ? Are ye daft ? Nane o' yer pawky humour at this time o' the day."

Often when we have decided on acquiring some good habit, say that of playing every approach shot to be passed the hole, the little voice of instinct upsets our plans. Referring to our opponent in the familiar manner as " he," "*He's* bunkered ! " the little voice will say, " Why risk going over the green ? Of course, my dear fellow, I realize what a fine thing it is to play to be beyond the pin, but on this occasion do listen to reason. Just a pawky chip, anywhere on to the green, down in two putts, and THE HOLE IS YOURS ! "

A great many golfers play in a careless, unreasoning way. They may hold a lead of three or four holes at the turn, and then their inherited instincts come into play. Like the cave-dweller who ceased to think of the future when his belly was full, like the Ojibbeway Indian who takes no thought of the morrow when he pitches his tent near the carcass of a moose, so the average golfer slacks off his play just at the time he should press his advantage home. Possibly he will be horribly annoyed when the match is lost, and will decide upon all manner of reforms, but these are soon forgotten.

Undoubtedly it takes some little effort to get out of the rut, and yet not very much, for the golfer has *desire* as the motive power to urge him forward, the strongest motive power in the world.

A German psychologist has suggested that the temperament of every one changes with their age, not

THE CONFESSION BOOK 53

slightly but radically. A child is sanguine; a youth melancholic; a middle-aged man is choleric; while an old man is phlegmatic. Can it be, I wonder, that every golfer passes through these stages? The beginner is usually sanguine until we tell him how difficult is the game he has elected to play; and when he has come to believe us, and finds the game absurdly difficult, he becomes melancholic, and there, in the majority of cases, he stays. He never progresses, remaining a melancholic golfer for the rest of his life.

But as I have said, the study of temperament, though absorbingly interesting, is of practical value only as a means of discovering one's weaknesses. There is a danger if introspection is carried to an extreme; to be conscious of oneself may lead to self-consciousness, and so, instead of helping a golfer to overcome his nervousness in driving off from a crowded tee, it would reduce him to a paralytic state of "funk." So the problem before the golfer is to find out his weaknesses, and to cease brooding over them, to stop worrying about them altogether, and to divert his energies to overcoming his faults.

If this book should fall into the hands of a golfer in his "teens," I would advise him to leave his temperament alone; tinkering with it would be dangerous. All the young golfer need worry about is to hit the ball hard, to strive to win every game he plays, and when he loses, to lose gracefully.

It is, to me, a matter of surprise that so few golfers keep any record of the matches they play. There is the classic Match Register of the late Lieut. Tate, some pages of which are printed in his "Autobiography," by Mr. J. L. Low, but beyond this no celebrated player appears to have kept any record, even of his important matches, or if such a record has been kept, it has not seen the light of day. I know of only one among my golfing acquaintances who has kept a complete record, and the battered old exercise book that he uses is the most valuable book in his library. True, a Match Register is hardly likely to improve a player's golf, although many of the matches in it may be a record of human failure and may remind the owner that his play at certain holes is invariably bad. But I do think that a Confession Book will help a player to discover his weaknesses, and so lead to their eradication.

Some years ago there was a confession book craze, but I am not suggesting that the golfer should obtain a leather-bound, parchment-leaved, beribboned volume in which to set down his golfing sins, nor that he should beat his breast, like Robinson Crusoe, and confess himself a miserable sinner, after every round he plays. But I do think it would be a good plan to write down a plain statement of his shortcomings as regards both the physical and the mental side of the game. Then he might analyse three or four rounds during the next month, and from this data he might draw certain conclusions. In a very short time he would have something definite to work upon, and at the end of each month he would be able to discover whether he had made any progress.

It is really very strange how many golfers cheat themselves: at the end of a round they calculate out that, roughly, they were 85, *if* they allowed themselves a five at such and such a hole where their opponent picked up, and *if* they had holed a putt or two which a generous opponent had given to them, and *if* they had taken six at the tenth hole instead of a seven;

THE CONFESSION BOOK 55

of course, had it been a medal round, they wouldn't have tried a long shot out of the bunker, they'd have used a niblick, just chipped the ball on to the fairway, played an iron shot on to the green and down in two putts. . . .

Says their opponent, to a sympathetic circle of players: " Pretty hot! 85 less 12 = 73. I can't give old Blank four shots if he plays like that. What the deuce are the handicap committee doing. Fancy giving Blank twelve when he plays down to six!"

This is the magic way in which an actual score of ninety becomes an eighty-five, and can there be any wonder that Blank is annoyed when his next medal card records 93 less 12 = 81.

I know very well that the suggestion of keeping a Confession Book will amuse many of my friends; but by any other name its practical value will be the same. It need not occupy more than half an hour of its keeper's time each week.

First, set down a statement about your tee shots: is accuracy sacrificed for length?; do you, at each hole, try to drive on a definite line? or are you content to be somewhere on the fairway? Assuming that you use a wooden club at fifteen of the eighteen holes, what percentage of these fifteen tee shots do you foozle? When the matter is reduced to hard figures, I think the average golfer will receive a shock, for three bad tee shots out of fifteen is twenty in every hundred, an absurdly high percentage, although I feel certain that 60 per cent would represent the average of many players.

This discloses a serious weakness, and whereas many golfers will argue that they know quite well that their percentage of " bad " tee shots is very high, I do not think that they realize how high it often is. In my youth I was told that dissatisfaction was essential to progress, and herein lies the value of the Confession Book: it will make you very dissatisfied with your golf. But if you are sufficiently keen on the game to analyse, and plot and plan, you are hardly likely to feel so utterly dissatisfied as to think that gardening is preferable to golf.

This analysing of the physical side is likely to afford some clue to the mental side. Thus, if your tee shots are bad, you are more than likely to be lacking in self-control, and by sacrificing length for accuracy you will gain not only accuracy but, naturally, self-control.

CHAPTER VIII

PUTTING AND AUTO-SUGGESTION

AT the present day no book on golf could be considered complete without a recipe for holing short putts, and, unless mention was made of the topic of the day, auto-suggestion. So why not combine the two ? or should I put it the other way round and say that good putting and auto-suggestion go hand-in-hand.

Every one has heard of Mons. Coué; we are all acquainted with the twenty knots in the piece of string, and if there is anyone in the country who has not repeated the phrase, " Every day I grow better and better," I can only suppose that he is so terrifically well that growing better seems impossible.

But kindly take notice, Courteous Reader, that this is a serious subject, and that the heights to which the man who practises auto-suggestion can reach are illimitable. And before you take the plunge and tie those knots, for heaven's sake acquire a sense of proportion, if you are not possessed of that sense already. You cannot grow a new limb, supposing that you have lost one, by auto-suggestion, or a new crop of hair, but you can train yourself to hole yard putts, or at any rate a high percentage of them.

The public interest in the lectures of Monsieur Coué was extraordinary, and there is no doubt that auto-suggestion will cure many mental and perhaps some physical diseases, provided that the patient is a firm believer in the probability of his cure.

The value of Mons. Coué's lectures was minimized to a large extent by the Press. Cartoonists found a butt for their drolleries; the funny reporter—funny as opposed to either witty or humorous—was in his element. Let me hasten to add that I realize the value of humour, yet I see no reason why a serious subject should be held up to ridicule by ignorant persons.

"Nevertheless, auto-suggestion is practicable, and though it may show meagre results to start with, the power to apply it increases with practice, and it has this decisive advantage, that the commands are our own, and not imposed upon us from the outside." Thus Doctor Wingfield-Stratford in the "Reconstruction of Mind."

Doubtless, you may wonder whether I practise what I preach. Let me set your mind at rest. I do! but, for once, I am not going to bore you with my own troubles. Besides which, the practicability of auto-suggestion is vouched for by numberless authorities. Mine is the task to set your footsteps on the right road.

There is little need to tell golfers how spontaneous auto-suggestion affects their play. At times, all of us have had a feeling that we are going to "sink" a long putt; we even pause when such an action would appear more than likely to be dangerous, and tell our opponent that we propose to hole out. And in the putt goes, I own not always, but in many cases it does go into the hole. That is spontaneous auto-suggestion.

PUTTING AND AUTO-SUGGESTION

Perhaps it would be better at this stage to state the difference between suggestion and auto-suggestion, because confusion has arisen in the past; even celebrated writers on golf have made mistakes. When a person insinuates a belief into his own mind, that is auto-suggestion; but when our partner in a foursome or fourball insinuates a belief into our mind—nonsense! you can't miss the putt—that is suggestion. The part that suggestion plays in golf is very great, but a discussion on its importance must be left to a later chapter.

In writing this chapter the story of the man who attempted to sell golden sovereigns at sixpence apiece in Trafalgar Square comes into my mind. I propose to sketch out a course of auto-suggestion and putting in the hope that you will give it a fair trial. More I do not ask, but I am very much afraid that you will not risk the sixpence, thinking my sovereigns are made of base metal.

Auto-suggestion appeals to or directs the imagination, and as I have already pointed out, the will yields to the imagination. At definite times in every twenty-four hours we relax the voluntary activity of the mind, we are but half-awake, and the mind becomes filled with a series of vague images. This is termed *the outcropping of the subconscious*. In some people this state is normal, and recurs with regularity, usually just before going to sleep, and in the morning just after waking. It is at this time that the straightforward formula must be repeated: Every day, in all respects, I grow better and better. The unfortunate golfer who does not fall into this state of suggestibility must cultivate such a condition by closing his eyes, relaxing his muscles, and allowing his mind to wander.

No attempt should be made to direct the thoughts into any particular channel, but if they do dwell on putting-green problems, so much the better. All this sounds a solemn, painful business, but it is very much easier than one would think, and since golden sovereigns cannot be obtained for sixpence every day of the week, it is worth while making a serious attempt.

Naturally, before repeating any formulæ, the golfer must make up his mind exactly in what way he wishes to improve, and although, so far as putting is concerned, he ought to have satisfied himself that the methods he uses, or the physical side of the " game within a game," are founded on correct principles, I do not think that this is of very great importance. There must be a desire to improve, and a knowledge of the ways in which improvement is possible. With most golfers this cannot present a serious problem ; they can improve their putting by leaving themselves little to do after they have made their approach putts, and by doing that little more satisfactorily than has been their custom in the past. Particularly would I warn them against that old and pernicious practice of playing their approach putts into an imaginary circle a yard in diameter, not because this method is unlikely to lead to the holing out of such putts, but because I am convinced that to attain accuracy one must putt at the hole. It is infinitely better to be a yard past the hole than eighteen inches short, for knowledge that you have given the hole a chance begets confidence in the return putt. In short, nearly every golfer can improve his putting by starting his approach putts straight at the hole, allowing, of course, for the contours of the green, and of sufficient

PUTTING AND AUTO-SUGGESTION 61

strength to be past the hole, and by playing his short putts to hit the back of the tin.

All that remains to be done is to keep these two means of improvement firmly in mind, to repeat the formula, and to feel certain that one's putting must improve.

In auto-suggestion itself there may be nothing new, but in M. Coué's method of conscious auto-suggestion, there is quite a lot that is new, despite what the newspaper reporter tells us. In the past, after a hard day's golf, we have sat in an easy chair listening to the wind howling outside and watching the flames from the fire dance up the chimney, and often we have said to ourselves, every time I play, my golf gets better and better! And when we wake up the next morning, and lie in bed half asleep, probably the same thought occurs to us. This is spontaneous auto-suggestion, and while it is going on, our imagination presents us with very vivid pictures of good strokes that we made in our last round.

So, obtain your piece of string, knot it twenty times, be clear in your mind of the *modus operandi*, repeat the formula, and every day, in all respects, your putting will grow better and better.

In saying that I do not think the physical side of putting is of great importance, I have in mind the epigram of Bernard Shaw : " The golden rule is that there are no golden rules." I never remember having seen a professional giving a lesson in putting, and I think that the attitude of most professionals would be that while they could teach one to hit a ball with a driver with fair accuracy, they could not teach one to hole twelve-foot putts.

Duncan mentions what he calls " a law of averages,"

which, he says, works out fairly certainly in putting. Let me quote from the book "Present-day Golf." "It may seem strange, but it is perfectly true, that when a man becomes a first-class golfer his putting becomes 'just average.' I have a case in mind. C. H. Mayo burst into golfing fame, as I did myself, in 1906, at Hollinwell, when he ran up Sandy Herd, in the 'News of the World' final. Now Mayo, in 1906, was not a first-class golfer, but he certainly could putt. . . . In time Mayo improved his general game. Then his putting became normal, and so it happens to most golfers."

Why should an improvement in a player's general game lead to a deterioration in putting ? I know that it does, because I have myself seen a remarkable instance of it. Six months ago, I regarded a friend with whom I play very often as one of the best, if not the best, putter in the world. Owing to a long illness his wooden club shots were very short, but his putting was extraordinary. It had to be, for the course on which he plays is well over 6,000 yards long, and is exposed to every wind that blows. This friend's game was a series of wooden club shots and long putts. At one particular hole which asks for two good strokes from an average mortal, he used to play short of cross bunkers with his second, follow this with a brassie shot of about 150 to 160 yards on to the green, and hole his putt for a four. But, as in similar cases his tee shots gained length at the expense of his putting, he remains a far better putter than the average, but no longer a "world breaker." Again, all that one can put this down to is a change of mental attitude. My friend played round after round, knowing that he *had* to hole his putts. To-

PUTTING AND AUTO-SUGGESTION 63

day putting is no longer of prime importance, I can think of no other solution.

Unfortunately, it is impossible to make much use of the imagination on the putting green; it is more difficult to visualize a long putt finding the hole than it is to imagine that Income Tax has been abolished. But what the player lacks in imagination he must make up in determination. If he cannot say to himself, the putt will go in, I can see it running up to the hole and rattling to the bottom, he must say, the putt has got to go in. At all costs he must avoid the thought, will the putt go in?

I must confess that the Russian Ballet style of putting which is so fashionable to-day, seems to be a very undesirable compromise. Obviously, the Pavlova-like attitude which some players adopt, is used for the sole purpose of keeping the body still. But to balance the weight so that all of it except one ounce is on the left foot—the one ounce is, of course, supported on the tip of the right big toe— appears unnatural; as much as to confess: unless I place my body in such a position that I simply cannot move it, I am unable to keep it still.

Never up, never in, is an excellent piece of advice. Every golfer should bear it in mind. Murmured quietly to one's opponent when he is short it is worth, at a modest estimate, two holes in every round!

Returning to auto-suggestion, I have previously said that I am certain that every golfer practises it spontaneously, but only in a haphazard, irregular way. Some, for a few minutes once a week, others, for a similar time once a month, and perhaps a very few practise it after every round, not immediately after the round, but when they are drowsing in a lounge chair after dinner.

Now, since the certainty of auto-suggestion cannot be gainsaid, it would seem that this theory of spontaneous auto-suggestion solves many subtle problems. Why does one golfer play better than another, when both have equal advantages? Why was it that Braid, Taylor and Vardon dominated the world of golf for so many years? Why Braid? Why Tayloy? Why Vardon? Why those celebrated three in particular? Why not three of the lesser stars whose names are forgotten to-day by the average golfer?

Courteous Reader, I can hear you say (and I hope I detect a little pity in your voice), My poor author! Have you never heard the word genius? Don't you realize that Braid, Taylor and Vardon are geniuses?

But surely genius is a power inherent in the Human Race. There is nothing mysterious about it, it is natural to man, and for all I know natural to dogs and cats, elephants and earwigs. It is simply an extraordinary, imaginative, creative, or inventive capacity. Doctor Wingfield-Stratford describes it as " the sudden outburst of what has been accumulated in the subconsciousness, just as the discharge of an arrow is the release of force generated by the drawing of a bow."

Twenty, thirty or a hundred years from now there will have to be bunkers in the air, golf courses will have to be reconstructed and lengthened, possibly players of the future will revert to the gutty ball, or a great, great grandson of Mr. Croome will perhaps invent, after many experiments, a new type of ball

PUTTING AND AUTO-SUGGESTION 65

having its centre of gravity nowhere near the middle; in short, some method will have to be discovered for stopping the millions of golfing geniuses from doing every hole in one. For millions of geniuses there will be when the trick of storing and releasing mental energy has been revealed.

Or will the world cease to play golf as a game too easy to be of any interest. And if such be the case, how our grandchildren will laugh when they remember that golfers played for two hundred years, pondered over the game, and wrote innumerable books, explaining how to play the game and how not to play it, but neglecting altogether the simple solution that to play golf well one just had to become a genius, a mere matter of a little auto-suggestion.

And despite the "slings and arrows" of my critics, I wish further to state that by auto-suggestion a player can train himself to keep his eye on the ball; without practising it, he may, or he may not, keep his eye on the ball.

CHAPTER IX

THE LURE OF LONG DRIVING

I THINK that the sensation or emotion of pleasure derived from a long drive is the keenest and most enjoyable in the whole game of golf. There is always a feeling of fear when a long putt is made, even though the ball appears to be running straight for the hole; fear that due allowance has not been made for the slopes of the green, or that a worm-cast may deflect the ball. One can never be quite certain that the ball is going into the hole; and if a long putt does find its mark the reaction, at any rate in my own case, leaves one feeling like a man who has passed through great perils, and thus it detracts from the enjoyment. But when one has timed a drive perfectly, when the ball leaves the club with that feeling of "sweetness" that it is impossible to describe, and continues to rise in the air defying the laws of gravity, there is no feeling of fear; and it really doesn't matter very much whether the ball lands on the fairway or plunges into a bunker.

That the cult of long driving is a snare and a delusion, newspaper correspondents have told us times without number. They muster all the arguments against the insane desire to hit the ball out of sight, but usually they spoil the excellence of their discourse by telling us that Mr. Slasher reached the green at a hole 487

THE LURE OF LONG DRIVING 67

yards long with a drive and a half shot with a light iron; and so, heedless of their arguments, and remembering that motto of our youth: "What man has done, man can do!" we determine to emulate the deeds of Mr. Slasher.

Although it is the wish of nearly every golfer to be able to drive a low ball that rises at the end of its flight, very few players realize why a golf ball rises during its flight, or rather, how it can be made to rise at the end of its flight. This depends on the ratio of underspin to the velocity at which the ball is travelling. A large amount of underspin, coupled with a low velocity, will give a ball that rises quickly during the early part of its flight, and the reverse is the case; a high velocity with little underspin, and the ball is not likely to rise when it has been in the air for some time because the underspin will have diminished. It is impossible to give any figures that would have any bearing on the ratio of underspin to velocity, so far as the rubber-cored ball is concerned, nor is it at all probable that such figures would help the average golfer. But as soon as a novice can make sure of hitting the ball with a reasonable degree of accuracy, he would be well advised to carry out a few experiments for himself.

During a full swing with a driver, there are some two or three inches on the path of the club's head when, if it meets the ball, the result will be a fair shot. In other words, if you tee up a ball, and after a waggle or two, take up your stance, supposing a friend moves the ball, provided he does not move it more than an inch, either nearer the hole or away from it, your stroke will still be fairly successful. But the amount of underspin will vary considerably. Move the ball forward and the underspin will decrease; until, if the ball is moved two or three inches, the club will strike it an ascending blow and impart topspin. Moving the ball backward will have a reverse effect, for the club will be descending on to it. By this it must not be understood that the farther the ball is moved back the better the stroke will be, but I feel sure that the beginner and the long-handicap player do not realize that an alteration of stance, with regard to the ball, has the effect of varying the underspin. The novice usually starts the game by adopting a stance that will assist him to lift the ball into the air; the ball is placed opposite or even in advance of the left foot, and while, by this means, the novice may find lifting the ball off the ground is easy, such a stance handicaps him and makes progress impossible. An hour or two spent in experimenting may make a big difference to the length of a golfer's tee shots.

In the chapter on the Eye and the Ball, I have said that few golfers can define the word *timing*, although there never is any doubt as to whether a stroke is, or is not, well timed. Here is another of golf's little mysteries: many golfers can time their tee shots without knowing how they do; it is not a question of their being unable to devise an apt definition to fit the word *timing*, they haven't the vaguest idea how they do what they do. I think the formula $MV^2 = mv^2$ will solve the problem. Being interpreted, mass of club multiplied by its velocity squared, equals mass of ball multiplied by its velocity squared. If we consider the mass of the ball and the club to be equal, the formula resolves itself into velocity of club equals velocity of ball. Hence the faster your club

THE LURE OF LONG DRIVING 69

is moving when it makes contact with the ball, provided the underspin is correctly apportioned, the farther the ball will go. Doubtless a mathematician would be aghast at this juggling with figures, but the fact remains that long driving does depend almost entirely on the pace, or velocity, of the head of the club. Of course, many factors have not been considered : much must depend on the shaft of the club, and on weight of the head : the elasticity of the ball should be dealt with. But as most golfers use one driver for all their tee shots, and more often than not, one particular brand of golf ball, two of the factors remain constant. So far as the weight of the club affects the length of the drive, it seems obvious that the heavier the club is, provided the player can swing it as fast as a light one, the greater will be the length of the tee shots. A distinguished golfer, whose name I cannot remember at the moment, has made the wise remark that few players experiment sufficiently with the weights of their wooden clubs. He contends that it is an easy matter to have the weight altered, and that it is only by repeated trials that a suitable weight can be found.

To return to the mysterious word *timing*. The number of muscles used in a golfing swing is enormous ; one would imagine that nearly every muscle in the body comes into play. But since mere brute strength will not achieve the same results as lesser power more skilfully handled, it would appear that the secret of timing, and so of long driving, lies in the proper co-ordination of the muscles. In some ways this contraction and expansion of muscles resembles the mechanism of a machine gun. It is difficult to make a novice understand the working of a machine gun because several things happen at the same time, and much the same difficulty confronts anyone rash enough to detail a swing at golf. It is not my intention to deal at length with the golfing swing, for this has been explained by numberless writers. But the novice who wants to go deeply into the matter, might consult James Braid's "Advanced Golf"; while for a simple explanation, Mr. Bernard Darwin's "Tee Shots" is excellent.

The secret of correct timing lies in the movements of the body. There is only one reason why the body is pivoted on the hips, and that is to allow a free swing of the arms. The ball can be hit a moderate distance without any turning of the body whatsoever, but in modern golf every yard from the tee counts, and a moderate distance is not enough. But the movements of the body must be regarded as auxiliary to the swing of the arms; and during the downward swing the body must be kept in check. The stroke is less likely to be an absolute failure if the body lags a little behind the arms; but allow it to take control of the swing, and drag the arms down to the ball, and the result will be a very short shot, pushed out to the right.

The formula which I have already mentioned proves, for all practical purposes, that length depends on the velocity of the club's head when it meets the ball, and since the movements of the body help or hinder the free swing of the arms, *timing* results from the proper co-ordination of the body with the arms. But how this helps one to keep one's eye on the ball, I cannot conceive !

How often one sees amateur golfers attempting to hit the ball "at the top of their swing." The pace

THE LURE OF LONG DRIVING 71

of the swing is increased during the backward movement and the club is jerked down towards the ball. If one asks a friend to lift a heavy object, such as a chair, it is curious to note that he will contract the muscles of his shoulders before he lays a hand on the chair. This is faulty muscular control, but the fault does not lie in the conscious mind. There are many parellel instances in everyday life : if you see a porter lifting heavy luggage, there is an inclination to contract the same muscles that he is using ; and particularly in a theatre, many members of the audience will unconsciously grip the arms of their seats during any tense moment in the play. The mere fact that a golfer knows that hitting a ball requires muscular effort, causes the contraction of the muscles. James Braid mentions the feeling of " tightness " that should be experienced at the top of the swing, but the tension must on no account be released until the club has started down. However perfectly the club is swung back, the whole success of the stroke depends on the beginning of the down swing. Start the arms down smoothly, let the body follow them, and the stroke will be well timed.

Undoubtedly the greatest pitfall in long driving is in playing for a hooked ball by " shutting " the face of the club. It is very easy to tell whether a player is shutting the face by the position of the toe of the club at the top of the swing. Normally, that is with the " open " face, the toe of the club is pointing towards the ground at the top of the swing ; with the shut face, the toe will be turned up to the heavens. And when the club meets the ball the face will be turned slightly over, imparting considerable hook to the ball, which will make it run a very long way. The difficulty arises in allowing for this hook, and if the right line to the hole is down the right-hand side of the fairway, then the ball must be aimed well towards the rough. Shutting the face when driving against the wind will produce a longer ball than will the open-face method. Doubtless there are some professionals who can play with either the shut or the open face at will; but the amateur golfer had best avoid shutting the face.

CHAPTER X

"JUST NOT" SHOTS

WHAT is a "just not" shot? The term explains itself: it is the stroke that follows an approach which finishes just not on the green; it is the stroke that leaves the ball just not dead; and thus it is the stroke that precedes a putt just not holed. In short, it is that irritating little shot played from five to ten yards from the edge of the green. A nerve-twisting, score-spoiling, match-losing shot, for the simplest of all reasons, that it can be played and played well in one-and-twenty different ways, and played badly in a hundred.

Only a few days ago, a very distinguished golfer remarked to me: "It doesn't matter very much if your iron shots are somewhat inaccurate, provided you hole out in two from five or ten yards from the edge of the green."

The psychological effect of out-driving an opponent, or of being out-driven oneself, has frequently been commented upon by every writer on golf, but few have mentioned the importance in both match play and stroke play of the just not shot. And, possibly in consequence, the average golfer has paid little attention to it.

One of the main difficulties of the stroke has seldom been realized. When a player is a hundred and fifty yards from a green he is satisfied with an approach that will leave his ball anywhere on the green and thus the allowable error is a large one. If he aims at the hole, his ball can finish from ten to fifteen yards away and his stroke will be successful. But when he is playing from just off the edge of the green for the stroke to be really successful, the ball must be played to within a yard of the hole, and the error has dwindled down to practically nothing. A slight mistake and the ball may run a yard or two beyond the hole; or the smallest error in judging the correct line and instead of curling in to the hole the ball may curl away and run out of safe holing distance.

Nearly every golfer—usually to his undoing—speculates on the probable result of each hole in a match before that hole is half played. If he puts his second shot somewhere near the pin, and his opponent fails to get on to the green, it is not unnatural to suppose that the hole is as good as won, and hence a perfectly played just not shot to within a foot of the pin will do more than halve, or possibly win the hole, for its moral effect on the match will be considerable.

The various methods that a player has at his command when playing these little strokes from the edge of the green, may be classified under three headings : pitch shots, pitch and run, and run-up shots.

The pitch shot, when the ball is played right up to the hole, can seldom be used because so much depends on the wind and the condition of the green. Unless the wind is blowing straight from the pin to the player, and the green is on the slow side, the pitch shot so far as the average golfer is concerned is dangerous. For the scratch or plus player who can hit his ball with a high degree of accuracy and impart a

"JUST NOT" SHOTS 75

maximum of backspin, the stroke is an excellent one, and yet from observation I do not think it yields so good an average result as the run-up pure and simple.

For the run-up the golfer has the choice of two clubs, either of which will make the stroke excellently; his putter and his cleek. For some obscure reason, using a putter when not on the green is thought by many not to be "cricket." Indeed I have heard it denounced in the strongest terms. I can only exclaim with the poet:—

> "What! is the jay more precious than the lark
> Because his feathers are more beautiful?"

Surely the object of the golfer in playing these short approach shots is to get his ball as near the hole as possible, not to lift it high in the air. Only a few days ago, the present holder of the Amateur Championship, Mr. Hunter, told me that he thought many players did not use the run-up as much as they ought to in important matches. And if that is true of some of our leading amateur golfers, it is also true of the average golfer. There is nothing to choose between a good run-up and a good pitch shot; both will leave the ball dead, but there is a vast difference between a bad run-up and a bad pitch-shot. To pitch the ball as opposed to running it implies the use of greater power; thus a half-topped pitch shot will go flying over the green, while a half-topped run-up is exceedingly unlikely to leave a player in bad trouble; more often than not the stroke, although badly played, will give a fair result.

And it is largely owing to the greater power involved

that the pitch shot becomes difficult to play in a very close match, and the run-up comparatively easy.

For running the ball most players carry a special club. At the moment the "push-iron" seems to have caught the popular fancy, and to have ousted the approaching cleek. But both these clubs have a considerable amount of loft, and thus, strictly considered, the stroke made with them is more in the nature of a pitch and run, unless, and this is a very vital point, the player deliberately turns over the face of the club as he hits the ball. In practice, this reducing the angle of loft works very well, but unfortunately most golfers are not content with adopting this method solely for running shots; they turn over—or should I say down?—the face of their mashie or mid-iron when playing a pitch and run. Or they turn the face of their mashie back to increase the amount of loft, this having the effect of increasing the backspin and stopping the ball quickly. In other words, few golfers, in making these just-not shots, play any club to its correct value, and thus they increase the difficulties enormously. It is no exaggeration to say that by altering the angle of loft one club becomes five, and if you multiply by five the number of iron clubs that the average golfer carries, it would appear that there is a choice between twenty-five or thirty clubs for playing these little shots. This is about ten times too many, for by Euclid's *reductio ad absurdem*, if a player had five hundred clubs to choose from he would never know which to use, neither would he be satisfied that he had the right one when he was going to play.

There is very little that can be said about the pitch shot that has not been frequently dinned into the

"JUST NOT" SHOTS 77

golfer's ear. The cardinal point of a good pitch is that the ball stops quickly. The less run after the ball pitches the nearer can the ball be pitched to the hole. Although I have mentioned it before, I think it advisable to repeat, that to make a ball stop quickly even the shortest of strokes must be played firmly.

In playing a pitch and run there must be a critical examination of the exact spot upon which the ball is going to pitch, and when the player has decided upon this spot, he must leave the hole out of his calculations. It is impossible to concentrate upon two things at once when playing a just-not shot. I think it was Vardon who suggested selecting a mark on the green directly in line with the hole, but only a foot or two from the player's ball, and then, neglecting the hole, putting over this mark. Psychologically, this is a sound method, provided the golfer does not allow his thoughts to wander from the chosen spot to the hole. He must say to himself : If I pitch my ball on this spot, or if I putt it over that mark, it is certain to finish near the hole. And since to pitch on, or putt over, a predecided mark appears easy, the stroke will be played with confidence.

In the "News of the World" tournament recently played at St. Andrew's, a remarkable feature was the pitch shots played by some of the leading professionals at holes where a run-up was clearly wanted. Even in the early spring, when there has been more than an average amount of sunshine, together with a drying wind, seaside greens become exceedingly keen, and naturally, a pitch shot is not only difficult but risky. On an inland course the greens seldom become very dry until the middle or end of the summer, so that the inland golfer can pitch his ball boldly up to the pin for nearly ten months out of the twelve. Besides this, the coarse texture of inland grass helps the pitch shot. It is no exaggeration to say that the majority of inland players do not know how to run their short shots.

CHAPTER XI

A VINDICATION OF THE THEORIST

VERY few people, whether they are golfers or not, realize that the mind cannot stand still. Even the most phlegmatic, unobservant man, is continually receiving new impressions. In the course of a single round all manner of new ideas enter the mind of every golfer, possibly leading him on to trying experiments, an alteration either of grip or stance, or, it may be, a deliberate attempt to slice or hook an iron-shot.

Every golfer is at heart a theorist. This, I am aware, is a dangerous statement, a statement that will be controverted by some of the able correspondents to the London Press, who make our breakfast a more enjoyable meal than it might otherwise be, and who doubtless cause many dignified business men to run to the station to catch their train. It is a dangerous statement, because one can have too much of a good thing, and because, so far as golf is concerned, it is terribly easy to theorize too much. To advocate, or rather to glorify, the theorist, is possibly as dangerous as preaching Bolshevism outside Scotland Yard. It would be as perilous to give a small, enterprising schoolboy a stick of dynamite.

But I am convinced that the golfing theorist has the best of it; he derives a keener enjoyment from the game when his risky experimental shots come off than does the phlegmatic golfer whose motto is safety first. And more than this: since the human mind cannot stand still, it is natural to theorize, and consequently, unnatural not to.

For too long the theorist has been under a cloud; he has been the butt of his fellow-golfers, and he has been held up to ridicule by writers whose mission in life, or so one must suppose from their written word, is to make us into a country of world beaters. . . .

"Nothing is constant but change!" so wrote Haekel. "All existence is a perpetual flux of 'being and becoming'!" That is very true of golf.

And not only cannot the golfer's mind stand still, but neither can his play. So many rounds a year may about leave a man playing just the same at the end of the year as he was at the beginning. An increase in the number of rounds, and more time devoted to pondering over the weak points in his game, and a golfer's standard becomes higher; the reverse is also the case: little play, little practice, and no thought, and down the standard slides, and up goes the handicap.

When a golfer's handicap becomes low there is a mysterious process involved termed "steadying down." Strictly speaking, it is hardly correct to say involved, because sometimes the process is not involved, and the player's golf never does "steady down." Nearly every one who starts the game as a boy becomes a low handicap player; possibly not a scratch golfer, but a two or three handicap player. But why some get down to scratch or even plus, and why the remainder stick at two or three, is to my mind one of the most debatable and interesting points in the game. In many cases these players have plenty of leisure, and

A VINDICATION OF THE THEORIST

perhaps they play too much; to some money is no object, they can buy all the clubs that they require or desire, they can practise with the leading professionals over a great variety of courses. Yet they never make their mark in the world of golf. Perhaps the single word "temperament" will account for the golf of many, and yet it seems inconceivable that a man can play golf for a number of years and not find out whether his temperament requires modification. And once that is realized, there is no reason why the modification should not be accomplished.

Really there is nothing so irritating and so thoroughly bad for one's golf as to fail at a particular time when one wants to play well. This is true of the plus player and the twenty-four handicap golfer alike. If there was a golfer who could always play well, one could understand him (or her) sneering at the theorist, but the dissatisfaction engendered by bad play must lead any normal golfer—by which I mean one of sound mental balance—into the realms of speculation. Why did I foozle my drive at the eighteenth hole when I was dormy one? Why do I so often fail at the critical phase in my matches? Why? Why? Why? There must be some answer to the question; some reason, obvious or obscure; but it is an answer that the golfer must find for himself—neither friend nor text-book can help him.

As an instance, the average player will be certain to find out sooner or later that he is incapable of playing short mashie shots, with back spin sufficient to stop the ball quickly. This is an exceedingly useful stroke that may have to be made several times in a single round, and it is a stroke that few golfers, with double-figure handicaps, can play with any degree of accuracy whatsoever. I have one particular friend in mind who has always scoffed at the theorist, and who has eschewed theory as he would the plague. He has accepted as an unalterable fact that it is impossible for him to stop a ball with a mashie, and hence there is a terribly weak spot in his game. Instead of pitching boldly up to the hole, he lofts his ball on to the near edge of the green, in the hope that it may stop running when it reaches the pin. The mental agony that he passes through in playing such a stroke is terrible to behold. Countless friends have told him of this joint in his armour, but their theories have fallen on deaf ears; he will have none of them. And as he scorns theories, so he scorns practice.

Returning to the average golfer and his incapacity for making this stop shot, I am certain that it is of infinitely more value to him to learn by theory and practice how the stroke is made than to have lessons from a professional. This must not be taken to mean that I am in any way opposed to professional instruction, quite the reverse; indeed, as I have already said, the beginner who tries to teach himself the game, instead of having a course of lessons, is making a very serious mistake. He is laying up a great deal of trouble for himself in the future. But I do think that there are some things that a player had much best learn for himself, when it is an act of wisdom to select a quiet corner of the links, and experiment in, for instance, these stop shots with a mashie or mashie niblick.

Really the golfing theorist should be beloved by the golfing correspondent, because not only does he read every word of every article that the latter writes, but he believes every word—for as long as a week at a time! Of course, it is simply a trick of the imagination. " B. D.,"

A VINDICATION OF THE THEORIST

or "A. C. M. C.," or "C. B. M.," or "G. W. G." tells us that our salvation in playing a half-iron shot is to "hit the ball with the back of our left hand." We read, and we believe. And when we come to make a half-iron shot, we know that we are going to be successful; we imagine the ball sailing towards the hole, rising gracefully into the air and dropping by the pin. Down comes our mid-iron with a thud on to the ball, and the stroke is successful, for no other reason than that we have imagined it successful, because we are incapable of doubting the success of the stroke. Possibly for five or six strokes in succession we play a perfect iron shot, we are filled with joy; never again are we going to play anything else than a perfect iron shot. We think we have discovered the secret of iron play; but alas! sooner or later our imagination fails us. We foozle once, and then twice, and the secret has gone.

But if we have to puzzle out for ourselves the principles of iron play, if we discover what we have been doing wrong, that knowledge stays with us, although in many cases we may have a relapse and have to rediscover our fault. This is where the Confession Book is exceedingly useful. Each golfer can record the cures for his individual ills, and whenever he is off his game he can refer to the book.

A round of golf is really a struggle against a terrifying horde of weaknesses. The golfer has to keep in his mind, perhaps I should say, uppermost in his mind, his numberless faults. He may have a tendency with his wooden clubs to allow his right hand to slip under the shaft, producing a paralysing hook; he may forget to hit through the ball; with his iron clubs he may have a number of faults that must be remembered and fought against if they are to be held in check. So far as my own experience goes, it is seldom that I play a good round without great mental strain ; unless I remember my weaknesses and visualize myself overcoming them, my golf is wretched. But whether this is so with other golfers I am unable to say.

It is hopeless to strive for perfection at golf. There never was, and there never will be, a round played without containing a single mistake. Certain weaknesses may pass ; the golfer will superinduce habits that will eradicate them. But others, possibly lesser weaknesses, will take their place. So the struggle will continue.

I fear that my defence of the theorist is but a weak one ; that my critics will tear it into rags. But the fact remains, unaltered and unalterable, that the human mind cannot stand still, that nothing is constant but change.

CHAPTER XII

A PHILOSOPHY FOR BUNKERS

IT has often been said that bunkers are not placed on golf-courses to catch bad shots, but to punish shots that are not quite good enough. The golfer, when he finds his ball deep in a bunker, should remember this sage remark, and draw much consolation from it. But does he ? Does one golfer in a hundred, or one in ten thousand ? I am afraid not. Like the ardent politician who damns the Government, not because it is a bad or corrupt Government, but because damning the Government is a popular pastime, so the golfer damns bunkers, not for fulfilling their purpose, but just because they are bunkers. Indeed, it has become a kind of ritual to use strong language when bunkered. Such a mental attitude is all wrong. At the very time when a golfer wants most to have himself in hand, to use all the mental faculties of which he is possessed, to plot and plan serenely, he flies into a rage. Of course, with the obvious result : seizing his niblick, the golfer rushes towards the bunker, leaps into it, as an old-time armoured knight would throw himself into the fray, and without a moment's thought hews the ball out of the bunker. Where ? Where, doesn't matter.

Whenever I think of bunkers, and of bunker play, I am reminded of that excellent piece of advice to young men : Get money, my boy, honestly if you can, but get money ! Not for a moment do I advocate that unique method of bunker play when the golfer takes a handful of sand and his ball in his right hand, and throws both the sand and the ball out of the bunker. My interpretation of the advice, when a player is bunkered, is : Get out, my friend, as far as you can, but get out !

If one could devise a set of rules applicable to all hazards, the set would, I feel sure, consist of four rules : first, get out ! ; second, get out ! ; the third also would be get out ! ; and the fourth would be get out on to a predecided spot that will make the following stroke an easy one.

Not very many years ago it was regarded as highly eccentric to use any other club than a niblick in a bunker. To-day, the reverse is the case ; the niblick is seldom used, except for very short shots. Naturally, the use of a heavy club with a great degree of loft on its face means that the ball will not go very far, and many players seem to avoid using such a club because the loss of a stroke is inevitable, or rather, appears inevitable. But the pendulum has swung too far ; there is far too much " vaulting ambition which o'erleaps itself " about the modern golfer's play. If the red-coated old gentleman, with his midget-faced niblick, did waste one stroke every time he was bunkered, the average player to-day, with his spoon or mid-iron, often wastes two or even three strokes. Consider the remarkable case of Abe Mitchell in the Open Championship of 1920 at Deal. After a shaky start in the third round, he was badly bunkered at the fifth hole from a poor tee shot. He tried to get out with a heavy iron and failed. The hole cost him eight valuable strokes.

A PHILOSOPHY FOR BUNKERS

Here we have an excellent problem in bunker play. The consensus of opinion was that Mitchell made a grave error in trying for too much, but there is the other side of the question, and to my mind the whole championship hung on that single stroke. Had it proved a success, Mitchell would have gone on his way rejoicing. He would have obtained that stimulus of which he stood in desperate need. A pawky stroke with a niblick would have left him still struggling to recover lost strokes; in a way, it would only have added to his burden. A good stroke, with a little luck, might have altered golfing history.

I fear, Courteous Reader, that I must inflict another rule for bunker play on you, and then I shall have done with rules. When your ball is in a bunker, or in a bad place in the " tiger country," count ten before you decide what to do. In the early days of the Great War, a party of infantry, commanded by a non-commissioned officer, were defending a village. As the Germans advanced the fire of the infantry became wilder and wilder, until the " fire effect " was practically nil. Although the enemy were within three hundred yards the N.C.O. gave the command " Unload." This was instinctively obeyed, and was immediately followed by the order " Load." Only by this drastic method were the infantry prevented from " getting rattled." But unfortunately the golfer has no leader to prevent him from playing his bunker shots before he has spent due time in considering the possibilities and the probabilities. That is why I suggest that he should adopt the old plan of counting ten before he acts.

Surely the most hideously tempting stroke in golf is where the ball is lying in a shallow sand bunker on the edge of a green. It seems the easiest thing in the world to lift the ball without touching the sand, and drop it near the pin. That it is not by any means easy is due to the absolute accuracy that is required; an error of one-half or even one-quarter of an inch, and either the ball will not rise in its flight, or else the unexpected resistance from the sand will rob the club's head of its velocity, and the ball will flop scarcely a yard in the bunker. But it is so tempting to try the stroke because the "explosion shot" is one that it is difficult to imagine successfully played. If a golfer hits hard, he expects his ball to go a considerable distance; and it is difficult to realize that most of the energy will be expended in the sand, and that the club will not be travelling fast when it reaches the ball.

Very many golfers have told me that they prefer to attempt to lift the ball out of a bunker without any more than grazing the sand, because they find it difficult to estimate how much to aim behind the ball in playing the "explosion shot." There is a simple method for overcoming this difficulty, and one that is useful in other ways; this consists of screwing the feet firmly into the sand. Not only is the density of the sand accurately judged, but the stance of the player is perfectly firm, and this is of great importance in bunker play.

There is a very common failing in playing an explosion shot that seems to have been overlooked by most writers on the game. Besides striking the sand well behind the ball, the club must be forced through the sand towards the ball. The shock of the club meeting the sand is unlikely to frighten the ball, although that is what one might deduce when watching many golfers play the stroke. Possibly it is needless

A PHILOSOPHY FOR BUNKERS 89

to add, that the golfer must visualize himself forcing the club towards the ball before he attempts the stroke.

I once heard a brilliant suggestion that it was alleged would turn golf into a money-making business proposition ; it was that a golf course should be built near London without a single bunker on it ! It was claimed that golfers would pay any subscription to become members, since they would be able to boast that they had gone round in seventy or seventy-five strokes. It was to be the easiest course in the world, no bunkers, no undulations, and, of course, no rough ! But instead of being the easiest golf course in the world, it would probably be the most difficult, for, as Sherlock says, the drive and iron shot hole that has an unguarded green, is one of the most difficult holes to play. There are no bunkers to help the golfer, nothing to give him any indication of the length of the second shot, or to help him in deciding as to the " line " to take. And not only that, but the bunkerless course would be terribly uninteresting and dreary to play upon.

It is only of recent years, dating from the coming of the golf course architect, who, since he does not play the game for a living, is termed, paradoxically, the " amateur " golf architect, that the construction of bunkers has received an adequate measure of attention. There are still hundreds of courses that are strewn with the most objectionable, unimaginative bunkers that it is possible to conceive. It has been argued that there is only one purpose for a bunker, to punish not-quite-good-enough-shots. It would be vastly interesting to trace the evolution of the bunker from the wind-swept patch of blown sand, covered with coarse grass, to the penny-in-the-slot type of bunker that disfigures most inland courses. It would be instructive, too. For it resolves itself into this question : Does a golfer derive greater pleasure in lofting his ball over a towering sandhill, than in making a similar stroke over, let us say, a row of jerry-built suburban villas ? And that question can be answered in the words of the golfer (history does not relate his honoured name !) who, when he had made a good stroke, would cry : Ha ! nicely over the burn that time ! And when he foozled (which we must hope was very seldom) : Caddie ! pick my ball out of that blank sewer !

Perhaps, after all, it makes little difference what a hazard is like, if a golfer is playing well ; it is more pleasant to play over a sandhill than a villa, but not very much more pleasant. But when playing badly, there can be no doubt at all that the penny-in-the-slot bunker becomes peculiarly objectionable. Foozle into Sandy Parlour, hurtle a new ball into the wastes of Sahara, and there is no feeling of depression, rather one hurries forward agog with excitement. There is something so tremendous about the second shot that one feels sorry for an opponent who has taken a safe line ; possibly, since success is hardly to be expected, failure is not so displeasing.

CHAPTER XIII

GOLF IN A GALE

ON the majority of golf courses, it will be found that the wind will help a golfer as much as it hinders him. The links of the Royal Cinque Ports Golf Club is a notable exception to this rule; but on other courses it has been my experience that, on the average, the wind will be behind for about six holes, against for a similar number, and across, from right to left or *vice versa*, at the remaining six. Therefore it is logical, though nonsensical, to argue that since the wind helps almost as much as it hinders a player, there should be no difficulty in playing in a wind, and that scores should be little, if any, higher. And nonsensical though such an argument undoubtedly is, there is much more truth in it than the average golfer cares to acknowledge.

One has only to play consistently on a seaside course that is celebrated—possibly it would be more truthful to say notorious or infamous—for its winds, and to watch the attempts of inland golfers, to realize that it is the golfer who beats himself and not the wind which beats the golfer.

It is surprising, to those who remember the floating golf ball, how far the modern ball will travel against a strong wind without any effort on the part of the player to keep it low. Given a well-timed drive I do not think the loss in length against a fair wind is much more than fifteen yards, that is, assuming that the golfer does not use any more than his normal power. But the inland player, unused to our sea-breezes, tries to bring off the double event : he tries for a low ball, and he puts much more than his normal effort into the stroke.

Sound methods that succeed in calm weather, will produce excellent results in the strongest hurricane. There is the secret of golf in a wind in a sentence ; and I would be content to leave matters at that, if I thought that anyone would believe me !

Let me anticipate your arguments, Courteous Reader ! You would remind me of the numberless chapters written by the leading golfers—oceans of ink on acres of paper !—upon altering the weight of the body on to the left leg when driving against the wind ; and on the right leg when driving down wind ; of holding the ball into the wind, with either a hook or a slice ; of playing push shots with a mashie, or a mid-iron, or a cleek ; together with much advice upon the weight of the wooden clubs for use against a head wind.

Surely it is a debatable point, whether or no this chopping and changing of methods is of the slightest value to the average player. But it is a point I have no intention of debating, and one that every player must decide for himself. I have only raised the question because it seems to have become a generally accepted fact that playing in a wind involves quite different methods from those which will give success when playing on a calm day. Nothing can be farther from the truth.

One not infrequently meets inland golfers who are spending their holiday at the sea-side, who are posi-

GOLF IN A GALE 93

tively amazed that they cannot play steady golf in a stiff breeze. It seldom occurs to them that their methods are all wrong; that they have been content to play sloppy iron shots up to the green with a loose swing; that the grass of the fairways at their home club on account of the coarseness of its texture has encouraged them to pitch all their short shots, thus leaving them totally incapable of playing an accurate run-up. In fact, the list of sloppy methods that will yield a fair result in calm weather might be extended indefinitely.

A much more interesting point, equally as important, is in the power used in a full shot played against the wind. Many golfers press, by which I mean, swing their club at such a rate that they lose control of it, with "malice aforethought"; they know that they are doing so. On the other hand, many press, unconsciously, snatching the club back as if they meant to hit the ball at the top of their swing. But if they ask you what they did wrong, they express great surprise when told; they imagined that they went slowly back. Here is our old friend, "subconscious, unreasoned desire"! And it is passing strange that the desire to drive a long ball against the wind should lead a player into committing a serious fault without his being aware of it.

For driving a low ball against a head-wind the customary advice—weight on the left leg—is rather misleading. Golfers are prone to overdo any advice that they may take; they try to keep nearly the whole weight of the body on the left leg, and not only is their swing cramped but pivoting on the hips becomes well-nigh impossible. This state of affairs can be overcome either by keeping a little extra weight on the left leg during the swing, or by transferring weight to the left leg at the top of the swing. Of the two, the latter is much the more difficult stroke to acquire, but when acquired, it is much more certain in its results. This matter is fully discussed in " Present-day Golf," by George Duncan and Bernard Darwin.

For driving down wind the average golfer would be well advised to use a brassie. The underspin imparted to the ball has considerably less effect, and so unless the ball is lifted into the air it will only carry a comparatively short distance. This is particularly true of a very strong wind when quite short carries become difficult, although there is a large amount of run to all tee shots.

It is a strong cross-wind that, to my mind, makes golf peculiarly difficult ; and, undoubtedly, steady golf under such conditions requires great skill. Mr. Hilton is famous for the use he makes of a cross-wind. In discussing golf some months ago, one of the younger, hard-hitting, generation of players paid a great tribute to Mr. Hilton's methods. He said that while he could out-distance Mr. Hilton in calm weather, in a cross wind he found himself from twenty to thirty yards behind after every tee shot. I think I am right in saying that Mr. Hilton makes use of the wind, not by holding his ball into it, but by slightly cutting his ball in a left-to-right wind, and by hooking, or, to use the popular expression, imparting slight " draw " to his ball, if the wind is from right to left. But to attempt to emulate Mr. Hilton, or to follow the teachings of another school who fight the wind by holding their ball into a right-to-left wind by imparting a trace of slice and *vice versa*, is beyond the skill of the week-end golfer. The golfer who can only play

GOLF IN A GALE 95

two or three rounds a week would do well to remember the sage advice of James Sherlock, who says that the straight forward shot will in the long run, always give the best results.

In the opinion of most golfers who play continually in winds either moderate or strong, the most difficult shot to play successfully is a full drive when the wind is blowing at a player's back. A gust is so apt to come at an unexpected time, and to throw the player on to his ball. I am inclined to think that a golfer with an " open " stance is less disturbed than one with a square stance. And, although a change of stance from square to open has the added advantage that the tee shot is likely to be slightly cut, which will add to its length, I hesitate to recommend any such change. It is difficult enough to make the correct allowance in a cross-wind without adding another factor.

I have already mentioned the necessity of choosing a " line " for the tee shot ; it is easier to imagine a drive played on a predecided line than it is to imagine one hit anywhere down the fairway. If this is important in calm weather it becomes doubly so in a stiff wind when so much depends on the placing of the tee shot. Often a green will have bunkers close to both its left and right side, as looked at from the tee, and if a player has placed his drive on the right hand side of the fairway, if the wind is blowing from right to left across the green, the permissible error is very small. The second shot will have to be directed at the right hand bunkers, and thus the allowance must be absolutely accurately gauged or the ball will not finish on the green. Obviously the player who has driven down the left of the fairway will not experience similar difficulty over his second shot ; he will be able to aim at some part of the green, and a shot less accurately played will stand a good chance of escaping trouble. Although this may seem an elementary point it is one often neglected.

CHAPTER XIV

THE PSYCHOLOGY OF MATCH PLAY

"WHATEVER you put into your book, or whatever you leave out," said a friend of mine, "for Heaven's sake tell us how to win our matches!"

That is easier said than done. There is no formula for winning matches; no recipe of Mrs. Beeton will meet the case. Take one average golfer; garnish him with abundant common-sense; rub in his own limitations; pour over him the sauce of imperturbability; serve very hot! No! that will scarcely do. I feel certain that this winning and losing of matches must be approached, as it were, from an angle; we must enfilade the good match player, and outflank the bad, and attempt to find out why one is good and the other isn't.

The elements that constitute a good match-player are well known. The ability to play his own game for better or worse; but since his weaker brethren must have a game of their own it becomes fairly obvious that the bad match-player is the man who is easily put off his game, or cannot reproduce it when he desires to most. Thus to win a high proportion of matches the golfer must find out and eliminate those little or big worries that affect his play.

Is this logical reasoning? Perhaps. Do you agree

with it, Courteous Reader? I must confess that I do not myself. There is a great deal more in match play than appears on the surface.

Let us begin at the beginning. You are sitting in the club smoking-room when there enters a man whom you know by sight. He may be twenty years your senior, but if his handicap happens to be higher than yours, he will sneak up to the nearest table, extract a match from the box, light his pipe, and then open fire with a few remarks about the condition of the course, the terrible effects of the drought, coupled with the customary growl about the really extraordinary methods of the Green Committee. He then deftly turns the subject and comments upon the golf of X and Y, and so gradually leads up to how you yourself are playing. That was a terrific second of yours at the third, he suggests; and while you are glowing with pride at his lavish praise he blurts out that his handicap is twelve, but he thinks that he could give you a game. *Noblesse oblige!* You can't say no. Although sometimes the ignorant little bounder whose handicap is scratch because in the dim past his ancestors preferred scratching pictures of reindeer on the walls of caves instead of going out and clubbing mammoths with axes of stone, and have thus endowed him with the instinct of attention to stationary objects —this is "drawing the long bow," it is the only explanation I can give for the handicaps of some people—drawls out the customary lie: I'm simply booked right up, what! But you, Courteous Reader, although your handicap may not have reached that magic back-mark, agree that on Tuesday next, or it may be Saturday, you will be pleased to play.

And here, long before the game is played, the

THE PSYCHOLOGY OF MATCH PLAY 99

psychology of match play begins. Rumours reach you that your opponent is not really twelve ; about fourteen is his mark ; or yes ! he calls himself twelve, but he used to be three, and by bribery and corruption has had his handicap raised to twelve. You will beat him easily, or your chance is compared to the snowball in Hades ; you don't stand an earthly !

Thus you start weighing the matter up ; you collect more evidence ; possibly you catch a glimpse of your future opponent actually playing a stroke. And it is more than likely that when the appointed time comes and you arrive on the first tee you have reached some definite conclusion. With about as much evidence at your command as has the hero who tries to write a life of Shakespeare.

Talk of the scandal that is created when old maids meet over a cup of afternoon tea, it is nothing to the tattle on the first tee of any golf course. Call the remarks you hear—and make—terminological inexactitudes, if you care to, call them whatever you like, but don't let them sink into your mind.

Consider the following, which I have chosen from a hundred common-place remarks : Yes, I am playing with Y. I shall get some fresh air and exercise and he will get my half-crown. No ! I am not playing golf this morning. I am giving B. half-a-crown to have the pleasure of watching him hit the ball out of sight. Z. insists on taking his three strokes. Old Shylock ! I can't possibly give them to him. Care to play for anything ? I know you'll win, I'm right off my game.

These, as I say, are real-life remarks—I have not invented them for any fell purpose. But just consider them in detail. If B. does attempt to drive the ball out of sight he is more than likely to find that he is three or four down at the turn. And "Shylock" may find that the three strokes that he is so grudgingly given are by no means enough. And the man who says that he is right off his game may be speaking the truth, or he may be lulling his opponent into a false security. Above all, beware of the opponent who tells you how ill he is feeling; play him for as little as possible, thus you will lose less.

How seldom it is that one meets an opponent who thinks, or rather declares, that he is going to win. At times one plays with a stranger who appears quietly confident that he will win: but more often than not, if a strange opponent says anything at all, it is to express a doubt as to whether he will manage to give one a game. Yet why should this be so? Do we never say we are going to win because we hope to catch our opponent unawares? Is it really the case that ninety-nine out of every hundred golfers prevaricate for the sole purpose of lulling the suspicions of their opponents? Heaven forbid! We speak in a jocular manner. We don't mean what we say. Our opponents do not interpret our remarks so literally. Well, well, I suppose that is our defence; but I should hate to see an astute K.C. tear it into rags!

I must confess that I think many of the chance remarks made on the first tee, or during the course of a match, have an exceedingly important bearing on the result. If you are an hypnotic subject, or one affected by the suggestions of an opponent, you must try to let these chance remarks pass through your mind like "water through a sieve." It is idle to maintain that suggestion, the imposing of a belief by a stronger upon a weaker will, does not play an important part in match play. Indeed, there is a classic instance of

THE PSYCHOLOGY OF MATCH PLAY 101

this. In an important match one player was holing his putts from all parts of the green. Said his disgruntled opponent, in quite a casual manner: "I can't make out how it is you hole so many putts with the extraordinary grip you use." Extraordinary grip! thought the other, Is my grip extraordinary? And, naturally, the next putt he had to play he was thinking more of his grip than of holing the ball. His putting suddenly broke down. That simple suggestion put him completely off his game. It was as effective as a dose of chloroform, or a blow with a sledge hammer!

I have already mentioned the habit into which many golfers fall of speculating on the result of a hole after the tee shots, or possibly after the second shots have been played. This is akin to attempting to solve a problem with insufficient data. Let us suppose that X equals the capabilities of a golfer, and that Y equals the capabilities of his opponent. Then the result of a match between the pair will be $X-Y=?$ But neither X, who does not know the value of Y, nor Y, who does not know the value of X, can solve the problem. Taking a very common example that happens in almost every round played, and the absurdity of speculating in the capabilities of an opponent is clear.

Suppose, at a hole about 340 yards long, your opponent hooks his drive after you have played your ball straight down the middle of the fairway, and, further, suppose that your opponent hooks his second some twenty yards short and to the left of the green, and that your second shot finishes a few yards short of the green. In a case such as this, the average player thinks to himself: I've got him! At the best he can only hope to hole out in five, and supposing—

which is very unlikely—that I fail to get a four, I still halve the hole. But the advantage gained by one player over the other, in this typical example, is at the most only half a stroke after the second shots have been made. And if this advantage is not doubled, so that it becomes a whole stroke, the hole will be halved, unless, as is often the case, the unexpected happens. The player who has hacked his way to the green via the rough, may put an approach shot dead, or hole a long putt. Now, the position will be absolutely reversed: the advantage will have changed hands, and the player who expected a win and was certain of a half, has to struggle to avoid losing the hole.

Very often such a hole is the turning point of a match. How did I get on with B? I lost, most unluckily! I was two up at the turn; at the tenth, I was on the edge of the green in two; and B, after three foozles, holed out from a dozen yards off the green with a chip shot! Holed out for a four! Of course, I took three putts, and was only one up when I was almost certain to be three up! Nothing went right for me after that. . . .

Few golfers realize that it is a fatal policy to play pawky when their opponent is in trouble, for nearly every player finds it more difficult to play pawky golf than it is to play his natural game. The reason for this is obvious: pawky play involves a change of method, possibly a change that runs counter to a habit such as playing a " spared " shot with a wooden club. When an opponent makes a mistake there is surely only one thing to do, and that is to play the hole as well as one is able, to administer the *coup de grâce* without the slightest hesitation. With many

THE PSYCHOLOGY OF MATCH PLAY

golfers the mistake of an opponent is a factor added to the difficulties of the game. They allow their imagination to run away with them. If their opponent tops a shot they wonder if they themselves are likely to top; if he hooks or slices, they imagine themselves hooking or slicing. Well, I have had my say about the imagination; control of it is the key to good golf, and I have no intention of repeating myself.

Broadly speaking, the play of an opponent affects most golfers in two ways : his methods of play, and the result of his methods. But further than this, we must consider the temperament of an opponent, not only his golfing temperament, but his attitude towards life in general. Since all types of men play golf the novice must expect to encounter : the chatty player, and his opposite, the self-centred or morose golfer ; that objectionable person who must hole every putt and jot down his own score and who regards the match as of secondary importance ; the bad-tempered man who throws his clubs about ; the fellow with some semi-permanent disability (say a sprained wrist), but who only remembers it when he makes a bad shot, the bad loser, the deliberate golfer (this is what he calls himself, other people call him confoundedly slow) and . . . but the list might be continued *ad infinitum*. As Archbishop Trench most truly said, we have more words in our language to describe the vices than the virtues. Possibly we need them !

It must not be assumed for a moment that the above list of players are persons best avoided. For these are the gentry against whom it is difficult to play one's usual game, and for this reason alone matches must be sought with them.

Consider a match against a deliberate golfer ; a

man who takes a dozen waggles and then, unable to make up his mind to hit the ball because he has not goaded his imagination into picturing a successful stroke, begins all over again. One feels inclined to cry : Hit it, man ! but once his deliberate methods become anything deeper than a matter for amusement, the match is as good as lost. Such a golfer is " very bad to beat." In a match-play tournament last year one of the competitors was extraordinarily slow. Curious folk timed him, and found that on the average he took twenty-seven seconds addressing the ball. As may be imagined he went through that tournament like a steam-roller, until—it seemed a miracle to his victims—he was badly beaten.

In reply to my question, the winner said : " Oh ! I saw I should be hypnotized if I watched him waggle, so I looked the other way and repeated poetry ! " What a novel method of match winning !

Concerning the deliberate golfer and the very quick golfer, there is a curious parallel in cricket. A batsman who scores at an average pace will often slog wildly when at the wicket with a very slow player, but I feel certain that a cricketer who abandons his usual method and tries to score off good length balls is well aware of the fact, while I am by no means sure that the golfer knows that he is taking a shorter or longer time over his strokes. I think many of us realize it too late in the game.

Undoubtedly it will be of advantage to any golfer to vary his opponents as much as possible and to play frequently with strangers. It calls for greater effort to play satisfactory golf under such conditions ; and since the converse is also the case, it is fatal to play only with one or two friends and to avoid strange

THE PSYCHOLOGY OF MATCH PLAY

opponents. Many golfers get into the habit of pairing always with a friend against whom they can play well with very little mental effort. In this connexion I heard a most droll explanation as to why two players always played together in Medal rounds. Said one of them : " Why do I always play with Blank ? Well, he talks about gardening, a subject in which I take no interest, and I find that his remarks don't sink in. Just a Yes and a No in the right places, and on he goes talking about parsnips and broad beans. It keeps my mind from thinking of short putts that I have missed, and brassie shots that I have foozled.

CHAPTER XV

THE PSYCHOLOGY OF MATCH PLAY

(*concluded*)

IT is a very true saying, if a trite one, that matches are won by playing a little better than one's opponent. Statistics prove that the majority of games are won and lost on the seventeenth and eighteenth greens, and that runaway matches, when one golfer plays above his form and the other below, are the exception and not the rule. It is also true that in losing a match a golfer more often than not beats himself; in other words, his defeat can seldom be attributed to the brilliant play of his opponent. From this it seems obvious that the golfer who can play his own game and is not perturbed by a display of fireworks from his opponent but plods steadily on, will win a high percentage of his matches. It therefore seems expedient to examine some of the causes that put a player off his normal game.

Paramount among these is to be outdriven from the tee. To say the least of it, it is exceedingly unsettling to be playing the odd to a very long driver time after time during a round; but if it were only unsettling it would not be so bad. Other forces than a little mental unrest are brought into play, particularly the instinct of emulation. This instinct is noticeable in

THE PSYCHOLOGY OF MATCH PLAY 107

children more than in adults. Two children will play most happily with, say, a golf club until a stranger stops to watch them. Then they both want it. It is not that the one who hasn't got the club desires to take it from his brother for purely selfish reasons, but that since his brother has topped the ball most successfully for at least ten yards, he wishes to emulate his brother, or possibly demonstrate to the onlooker that he, too, can top the ball just as well.

Doubtless the instinct of emulation is a very useful one, but it is a poor policy to allow it to gain control during a round of golf with a long driver. So the player who is hitting his average length and yet is being consistently outdistanced must just "grin and bear it." He must adopt a philosophical attitude; and argue, firstly, that his opponent may try to increase the distance between the two drives, so bringing about his own destruction; and, secondly, that the long driver will always expect the advantage he is gaining to have a psychological value, and to cause his opponent to press. Really there is nothing so annoying as consistently to outdrive an opponent, and to find that the dolt doesn't seem to care a snap, but keeps plugging along down the middle of the fairway.

Sometimes one sees a short driver deliberately turn his back on his opponent. This, to say the least of it, is excessively rude, and moreover it fails to achieve its purpose. That can be stated without fear of contradiction. A stout-hearted golfer of my acquaintance acquired the extraordinary habit on the putting green of gazing with a rapt expression at the sky whenever his opponent was holing a short putt. Having given this unique method a trial, I know that it increases the mental strain, hence it is undesirable. For while mental strain cannot be avoided, it is folly to squander one's resources unnecessarily.

Attention has been drawn to the short-sightedness of expecting an opponent to make a mistake; sooner or later he probably will, but to rely upon his doing so weakens one's capacity for taking advantage of his error when it does occur.

An eighteen-hole match between two average golfers can be divided into three phases. The first would cover the beginning of the game, say the first six holes, when neither player has settled down, and when, through stupid mistakes on the part of either, holes change hands one after the other. Then both players realize that they have been playing somewhat slackly, and that nearly a third of the round is over. The man who is up, thinks to himself: "Here! I'm only two up and I ought to be four or five up. I must hang on to my lead." Thinks his opponent: "What an ass I've been! True, I am lucky not to be more than two down, but I might, had I but played steadily, have been one or two up!" So comes the second phase: there is what can best be described as a tightening up on the part of both players; mistakes become less frequent. At the end of six or seven more holes the match passes into its third, or critical phase. Now the player who is down realizes that he must play his best golf if he is to stand a chance of winning; that the time has gone by when a mistake can be permitted; that the loss of a single hole will make his opponent "dormy."

And, strangely enough, it is at this phase of the match, that the golfer who has been playing slack golf produces a few good holes. Possibly he regains the

THE PSYCHOLOGY OF MATCH PLAY 109

lost holes, and pulls the match out of the fire. But more often than not these good holes are his "swan song," an unavailing attempt to stave off defeat. But whichever way the match ends you will hear him telling friends all about it. He was three down and four to go, and actually squared the match at the seventeenth, only to lose the last hole; or, It was a magnificent game! He won all the last four holes and the match!

This arbitrary division of matches into phases is for the sole purpose of illustrating two points. That the first four or five holes of a match are of vital importance; and that few golfers try hard enough until the match is almost lost.

A good match-player is assuredly not the man who can pull himself out of tight corners, but the man who plays steadily throughout the whole round, and so does not get into tight corners. In one club of which I was a member there was a curious superstition that the player who won the first hole always lost the match. An examination into the minds of people who believe this superstition might prove of absorbing interest; but to the student of Abnormal Psychology, not to the golf player! However, in this connexion it is amusing to notice that the golf of many players improves when the "turn" is reached. It would appear that to some there is a mental connexion between the turn in the round and the turning point in the game. And very often the tenth hole is the turning point in a player's golf. The slate is, as it were, wiped clean at the end of the ninth hole. But, unfortunately, when we are playing slack golf, we defer the effort to improve until we reach the ninth hole, and then, when that has been played and we start the journey home, our play improves. More often than not too late!

I can only suppose that it is a question of stimulus; but it is also a question of habit. Clearly of bad habit. To defer any attempt to improve until the tenth hole, supposing one is two or three down at the sixth or seventh, is tantamount to throwing away more than one hole.

Concerning the golfer's " swan song," the spurt near the end of the game, no textbook, no written word, will help such golfers. The remedy lies in their own hands, nor do I think they will find it difficult to discover.

Very often one meets players who " fade away," whose golf goes hopelessly to pieces near the end of the round. These are the reverse of the mentally inert golfer : since not only cannot they raise a spurt, but their play becomes wild in the extreme. Their trouble is that they worry too much. Only last night I heard a man say that the chatty golfer worried him ; but ·I do not think the chatty golfer worries one so much as destroys one's peace of mind by his interminable small-talk. Worry is not the facing of an unpleasant fact; but the uncertainty about it. You cannot be worried about the amount of your income tax, but you can be worried by the uncertainty as to whether you will be able to pay what is due when the final notice is presented.

At the critical phase in a game the golfer's thoughts see-saw backwards and forwards : Shall he take his brassie and go for the green ? Would it be best if he used a mid-iron, and played short, relying on a good approach shot to give him a four ? The whole attitude of the man who " cracks " expresses uncertainty, and

THE PSYCHOLOGY OF MATCH PLAY 111

not only is he worried about what he ought to do himself, but he allows the play of his opponent to become of vital importance. He speculates about his opponent's play, even as far as calculating out what his opponent may or may not do, and, naturally, putting as gloomy a construction on it as possible. A see-sawing of the thoughts utterly precludes any such thing as mental concentration, because there can be no singleness of purpose. Manifestly the player who is worrying about what his opponent may do, and about what—if the worst comes to the worst—he may do himself is quite unlikely to play his ordinary, steady game.

Not long ago, I played a series of matches against a man who was an exceedingly sound player except in a close finish. He was receiving three or four strokes, and although the last of these came at the sixteenth hole, if there was only one hole difference between us when the fifteenth was played he was beaten. Very often he had only to play the sixteenth hole carefully to become dormy two. But he couldn't. He worried himself out of making any use of his stroke. Curiously enough, this sixteenth hole was much in favour of the player receiving the stroke; it was extraordinarily difficult to reach the green in two, while it could be reached in three average shots by most golfers. But that made no difference to my opponent; even as I write I can picture his face and realize the mental struggle that was going on in his mind. It is more than probable that he told himself that he *must* get on the green in three strokes; that he had got to. Possibly he even went so far as to picture himself playing his iron shot boldly past the pin, and then attempted to visualize the downhill putt which he would have, and which he must put dead. That assuredly is not the way to win matches.

In descriptions of golf matches one often reads that Mr. So-and-So is a very determined player, that he waggles his club in a very determined manner; in short, one pictures him exuding determination. But I can assure the golfer, and particularly that unfortunate class of player who " fades away," that determination is of very little use, if it is of any use at all. That phrase which is popular at the present day, The Will to Win, is humbug, it is clap-trap of the very worst kind. For the will yields to the imagination, and the player who " cracks " at a critical moment allows his imagination to " run away with him."

Sometimes you will see a player use a driving iron or a mid-iron on the tee at the critical phase of a match. And if he is successful he will most probably remark that the proof of the pudding is in the eating; and, so far as that particular match is concerned, he is perfectly correct. But deliberately to handicap oneself in such a way must lead to a weakening of one's powers. The use of the mid-iron where the driver is clearly the right club to use is in itself a confession that all is not well.

The golfer who " fades away " can hardly expect to overcome his weakness in a few rounds, but if the duration of his " cure " depends upon himself, the cure itself is straightforward. He must attempt to concentrate on each separate stroke, and at all costs avoid the error of trying for too much. He must remind himself that the hole he is about to play is, let us say, 450 yards long, and that all he can hope to do is to have a putt for a four. Then, without any

THE PSYCHOLOGY OF MATCH PLAY

pondering over the second shot, he must decide where to place his drive, and instead of adopting any pawky methods he must play a steady drive, just his normal swing, no attempt to force the stroke, or to spare it. His second shot must be played in precisely the same way, and even supposing that his opponent reaches the green in two, he must not change his plans and try for a long brassie shot that is beyond his power.

How easy it is to give good advice! and how difficult to take advantage of it! Those "little cords, or brakes," will weaken the wretched golfer's singleness of purpose, they will prove a drag on him, not once but a dozen times; but if only he sticks to it he will find his play improving, until, at last, he will be able to play his normal game under any circumstances.

Strange as it may seem, the most disconcerting thing to many players is to obtain a big lead in the first nine holes. So bewildering is it that the man who is five up at the turn is filled with awe at his own ability. He wonders how he has done it, or he goes to the other extreme and decides that golf is a ridiculously easy game. And while he is pondering over these matters his lead vanishes.

The whole art of match play can be reduced to a sentence: Play each stroke well within your power to accomplish a definite object, and strive to increase your abilities when out practising, not during a match.

CHAPTER XVI

CONCLUSION

WITH this chapter my task ends. It has, in the main, been a pleasant one, although there have been times when I feel that I have left unsaid those things which I ought to have said. If it has been a difficult task, that is the fault of the Psychologists, who have, it is to be feared, little time to worry over the troubles of the golfer. And, besides, they will invent such awe-inspiring terms for quite simple actions. But if my suggestions will help the average golfer to improve his play, and possibly set other minds puzzling over the same problems, then I shall be well repaid.

I am indebted to various friends for valuable suggestions and for advice, and to the editors of the *Daily Mail* and *The Golf Monthly* for permission to reprint the substance of articles contributed to their papers.

There is one problem—possibly the greatest of all—of which I have made no mention. That is the relation of the mind to the body, or, so far as we are concerned, the relation between the mental and the physical sides of the game of golf. Nor, through lack of knowledge, have I been able to carry out one valuable suggestion, which was that I should write a chapter on the Dietetics of Golf, explaining, among other mysteries, why one

CONCLUSION 115

glass of port will sometimes make a golfer play vile golf, when after two glasses he will play exceedingly well.

About the imagination I have said very much, yet nothing at all about the developing and training of it. But golf trains the imagination whether a player wants it trained or not. Can you read the reports of an important match without picturing the incidents described? And what is the golfer doing when he explains every detail of his last match but training his imagination? Boring his listeners he may be, but when he tells you, with graphic gestures, possibly swinging your poker round his head, how he carried the cross bunkers at the tenth in the teeth of a howling gale, he is living his round, shot by shot, over again, and that is the best of all methods of training the imagination. And if he does bore you, if you are so utterly lacking in sympathy that you cut him short, taking the wind from his sails by saying that *you* found no difficulty in carrying those same cross-bunkers, and further, that you used a light iron and not a brassie, then I fear that you will never make much of a golf player. For sympathy is but a branch of the imagination.

When a golfer ceases to be a novice I am inclined to think that he does not use his imagination for the sole purpose of visualizing any individual stroke, or perhaps he extends his mental activities and imagines himself overcoming his own particular weaknesses as well as making a successful stroke. Every player has some besetting sin; it may be bending the right knee at the top of the swing, and consequently dropping the right shoulder, or not hitting through the ball, and I think he uses, or ought to use, the imagination to keep whichever is his particular sin in check. He may make a very bad start to a round, and after a hole or two find out what he is doing wrong, and he will overcome this fault by having a practice swing and by using his imagination to help him. "That is what I am doing. This is what I want to do!" he says to himself; and he had better add, "This is what I am going to do!"

Reverting to the relation between the mental and the physical sides of the game, a friend has brought forward a diverting argument about the imagination. He says that players often slice the ball during a round without their having imagined that they were going to do so. I cannot remember his actual words, but I think he went further than that, and said that it was possible to hook or slice a stroke badly even when one had pictured a perfectly straight shot. But good golf demands more than a well-trained and well-controlled imagination; sound mental methods can never wholly make up for bad physical ones. If a golfer develops a chronic slice, due to, say, a faulty grip or stance, no juggling with the imagination can overcome it.

But let us leave the imagination and discuss, for a few minutes, that dreaded golfing disease which is termed "staleness." Here, again, we have a remarkable instance of the grotesqueness of golfing nomenclature. When a player is right off his game, when his play grows worse and worse, we say he is stale—if you thought for a week on end you couldn't find a more misleading word to describe the facts of the case. Perchance we say that such a man is "over-golfed"; but whatever we do say we carefully avoid any mention of the mind. And that, of course, is the root of the trouble.

CONCLUSION

Certainly we know little about the mind of man, but what little we do know we might try to turn to our advantage. We acknowledge the ills of the flesh, but there appears to be something dishonourable in the ills of the mind.

Every golfing stroke involves a complex mental process, a change or alteration of tissue; exactly what takes place matters not at all, but there must be a wastage, a using up. You strike the head of a match against the box; it flares up, igniting the wood; you light your cigarette and fling the match aside, it has fulfilled its purpose. Or you tee up and drive a dozen balls one after another, when practising, but you could not repeat the process, there must be a period of recuperation, a building up. The "used-up" golfer, so I prefer to describe him, must on no account lose his confidence in his own powers, for he is suffering simply from an illness of the mind. I do not think that he need give up the game, provided he learns to play left-handed. Every golfer, however badly he may play, has theories about how the game ought to be taught! If only he could retain the knowledge that it has taken him years to acquire and forget his own weaknesses and bad golfing habits, and, wiping the slate clean, use this knowledge to teach himself the game from the very beginning, what a player he would become! That is an idea that we all of us possess, deep down in our hearts. Well, here is the opportunity: learn the game left-handed. Choose one of the periods of mental "dryness," and bear in mind that not only is the ability to play a stroke left-handed of very great use, but that a new, and one might say unexplored, portion of the brain is being developed. It may be that in doing this the golfer will refute the time-honoured theory that since the full stroke is the easiest of all the golfing strokes it should be learned first. Certainly I would recommend any who uphold this theory to buy two left-handed clubs, a brassie and a mashie, and try for themselves ; perchance they will find reason to alter their views.

And now, Courteous Reader, let me make my final confession. I have pictured the average golfer as a man of many vices and few virtues ; I have suggested that he modify his temperament, instead of allowing the game to modify it for him ; that he sublimate his passions ; and that if he cannot control himself he cannot expect to control his club ; I have scoffed at his superstitions ; and made a mockery of the good resolutions that he makes, and breaks. All this, when I know quite well that if, by a freak of Nature, there ever arose a Perfect Golfer, he would have to give up the game because no one would play with him. Neither you nor I would care to play with a superman who never made a mistake.

But surely it is better to chase the will-o'-the-wisp of unattainable perfection than to strive after a lesser ideal.

INDEX

Andersen, K. T., on mental concentration, 50
Attention, psychology of, 17
—, Bagley, W. G., on, 18
—, controls movements of arms, 22
—, cannot become a habit, 23
—, forms of, 25
Auto-suggestion, spontaneous, 63
Average golfer, cheats himself, 54

Braid, James, 42, 71
Bunkers, object of, 84
—, rules for golfer when bunkered, 85
—, explosion shot, 88
—, golf course without bunkers, 89

Cortical cells, 12
Coué, Mons., 57

Darwin, Bernard, 70, 94
—, Charles, characteristic symptoms of Rage, 45
—, —, on the power of the force of habit, 27

Deliberate golfer, difficult to beat, 103
Desire, subconscious, unreasoned, 47, 93
Duncan, George, 25, 62, 94

Experience, 12

Gore, Major the Hon. J. W. W., 52
Greenwood, G. W., obliteration of bunkers from the mind, 37
Genius inherent in the Human Race, 64

Habit, 27 et seq.
Haeckel, 1, 80
Hesitation, 12, 14
Hilton, H. H., making use of the wind, 94
Huxley, J. S., 28

Imagination, 15, 116
Instinct, 51 et seq.
Introspection, 53

Keeping the eye on the ball, exercise in, 23
Keep yer e' a' the ba', 20

Long driving, underspin, 67

Mackenzie, Dr., erroneous ideas concerning the imagination, 15
Match play, phases of, 108
Memory, 7, 13
Mental attitude, in short putts, 4
— — of average golfer, 10
— — when practising, 14

Nerve force, 7

Open stance, in a wind, 95

Pawky play, 102
Practice, 22 et seq.
Practice swing, value of, 14
Psychology of match play begins before match is commenced, 99
Putting, mental processes in, 6

Shut face, 71
Singleness of purpose, 11

Slicing, cure for, 31
Speculation, dangers of, 5, 101
Subconscious mind, 50
— —, outcropping of, 59
Suggestion, 100

Temperament, 25
—, fundamental, 41
—, ideal, 42
—, definition of, 43
— can be modified, 44
— in match play, 103
Terminological inexactitudes, 99
Theory, dangers of too much, 79
Timing, 21, 69

Worry, 110
Watts, Dr., 4
Will yields to the imagination, 37
— to win, 112
Wingfield-Stratford, Dr., 11, 58, 64

For Product Safety Concerns and Information please contact our EU representative GPSR@taylorandfrancis.com
Taylor & Francis Verlag GmbH, Kaufingerstraße 24, 80331 München, Germany

www.ingramcontent.com/pod-product-compliance
Lightning Source LLC
Chambersburg PA
CBHW061418300426
44114CB00015B/1977